ВН

English Start

ACKNOWLEDGMENTS

The author would like to thank the following persons for their kind contributions:

Chiselle Armstrong and Kearne Peterson of Docucentre

Folke Wulf, manager, Canon Photo database WWF International

Matt Mattox of TechnologyReview.com

Steve Nelson

Tradewind Tours Jamaica

Amando Formaro of FamilyCorner.com

Marty Casado of Casado Internet Group

Christine Field of the Old Schoolhouse

Jeanette Hurtado of Enjoy Corp.SA

NIAid Office of Communication and Public Liaison, USA

Brian Loffler, marketing manager, New Internationalist Magazine

Robert Holmen of Trade Wind Tours Jamaica

iuniverse.com

English Start

English as a Second Language for students and adults

An Interactive Approach to English Language Learning

yasmin esack

iUniverse, Inc.
New York Lincoln Shanghai

English Start
English as a Second Language for students and adults

Copyright © 2004 by yasmin esack

iUniverse books may be ordered through booksellers or by contacting:

iUniverse
2021 Pine Lake Road, Suite 100
Lincoln, NE 68512
www.iuniverse.com
1-800-Authors (1-800-288-4677)

ISBN-13: 978-0-595-32752-2 (pbk)
ISBN-13: 978-0-595-77557-6 (ebk)
ISBN-10: 0-595-32752-4 (pbk)
ISBN-10: 0-595-77557-8 (ebk)

Printed in the United States of America

CONTENTS

Introduction ix

Chapter 1   Identifying and Communicating 1
               Locating Addresses
               Dates and Numbers

1.0   Looking at the Parts of Speech: A Review 1
1.1   Looking at Nouns: A Review 4
1.2   Conjunctions *And, But, or Nor*: A Review 7
1.3   *A, An, The*: A Review 9
1.4   Looking at Verbs: Present and Past Tense .10
1.5   The Present and Past Continuous *-ing* Endings 13
1.6   Using the Irregular Verbs 16
1.7   The *-ed* Verbs 19
1.8   The Active *-ing* and Passive *-ed* Forms .23
1.9   Using the Negative: *Not* 25
1.10   Noun and Verb Agreement 27
         1.10.1   Singular and Plural 27
         1.10.2   The Irregular Cases 29
                     Using Non-countable Nouns
                     Time and Distance
                     Collective Nouns
1.11   The Interrogative Forms 32
1.12   Conversation 1. Personal Identification 36
1.13   Conversation 2. Greeting and Introducing .38
1.14   Conversation 3. Meeting Friends 42
1.15   Role Play: Dealing with the Situation 44
1.16   Days of the Week, Months of Year, Numbers, Addresses 45
1.17   Using Prepositions: Locating Places and Dates 47
1.18   Student Dialogue 49
1.19   Script 1. Dates, Places, and Numbers. 51
1.20   Script 2. The Life of Sir Isaac Newton 52
1.21   Reading Comprehension: Save the Gorillas .53

1.22   Writing Skills 55
1.23   Review Exercises 57

Chapter 2   Describing 62
                Comparing
                Locating

2.0   Replacing Nouns with Pronouns 62
2.1   The Subject, Object, and Possessive Pronouns .62
2.2   Pronoun Agreement 64
         2.2.1   Agreement with the Singular and Plural 64
         2.2.2   Agreement with the Collective Noun 65
         2.2.3   Agreement with the Indefinite Pronoun 66
         2.2.4   Agreement with the Indefinite Pronoun and the Antecedent . . .67
2.3   The Reciprocal Pronouns 69
2.4   The Reflexive Pronouns 69
2.5   Prepositions and Object Pronouns 70
2.6   The Interrogative Pronouns 71
2.7   The Demonstrative Pronouns 71
2.8   The Relative Pronouns 72
2.9   Student Dialogue 75
2.10   Reviewing Adjectives 77
2.11   Using the Adjectives of Comparison
         The Positive, Comparative, and Superlative 80
2.12   Using Adverbs 83
2.13   Student Dialogue 85
2.14   Describing the Family 87
         2.14.1   Using Adjectives and Adjective Clauses 87
         2.14.2   What Do They Do? 91
         2.14.3   Family Activities 93
         2.14.4   Likes and Dislikes 96
2.15   Conversation 4. Talking about the Family 100
2.16   Writing Skills 102
2.17   Identifying the Items in the House 104
2.18   Prepositions 108
2.19   Student Dialogue 112
2.20   Describing the House 114
2.21   Conversation 5. Describing the House 117
2.22   Role Play: Dealing with the Situation 119

2.23   Reading Comprehension 122
         2.23.1.   Work Begins at Home 122
         2.23.2.   The Boy from Bogota 122
         2.23.3.   There Is a Mouse in My House 124
2.24   Creating an Advertisement 126
2.25   Scripts 3, 4. Floor Plans. 127
2.26   Review Exercises 129

Chapter 3   Time and Weather 132
                     Expressing Ability/Politeness
                     Adverb Clause of Time, Cause and Effect
3.0   Time and Weather 132
3.1   Expressing Time 133
3.2   Describing the Weather 136
         3.2.1. Using the Verbs 136
         3.2.2. Using Adjectives and Nouns 136
         3.2.3 Using Comparatives and Superlatives 138
3.3   Non-Countable and Countable Nouns: Describing the Weather 141
3.4   Student Dialogue 144
3.5   Expressing Ability and Politeness 146
3.6   Conversation 7. Expressing Time and Weather 151
3.7   Student Dialogue 153
3.8   Outdoor Activities 154
3.9   Let's Read: The Geography of Peru 157
3.10   Introducing the Adverb Clauses of Time 160
3.11   Introducing the Adverb Clauses of Cause and Effect 162
3.12   Conversation 8. Accepting and Refusing Invitations and Expressing
         Politeness and Ability 165
3.13   The Future Tense 170
3.14   Written Exercises 174
3.15   Role Play: Dealing with the Situation 176
3.16   Scripts 5, 6. 178
3.17   Review Exercises 179

Chapter 4   **Around: Requesting and Giving Information** 182
                Locating People, Things, Places
                Prepositions: *Next to, Near*
                Adjective Clauses: *When, Where*

4.0   Identifying the Neighborhood 182
4.1   Asking for and Giving Directions 186
4.2   Locating People, Things, Places
        Some Commonly Used Prepositions 187
4.3   How Can You Get There? 189
4.4   Student Dialogue 190
4.5   Conversation 9. Asking for Directions 191
4.6   Conversation 10. Getting around the neighborhood 195
        4.6.1   At the Bank 196
        4.6.2   Conversation 11. At the Clothes Shop 201
        4.6.3   Conversation 12. At the Shoe Shop 204
        4.6.4   Conversation 13. At the Grocery .205
4.7   Using the Adverb *Where* in an Adjective Clause 207
4.8   Using the Adverb *When* as an Adjective Clause 209
4.9   Noun Clauses 210
4.10   Student Dialogue 212
4.11   Role Play: Dealing with the Situation 213
4.12   Let's Read 214
4.13   Written Exercises 216
4.14   Script 7. The Future of Communications 217
4.15   Review Exercises 219
4.16.   Pronunciation 224
        4.16.1   Pronunciation of the -ed words 224
        4.16.2.   Pronunciation of the -es and -s words 225
        4.16.3   The Silent *w* 225
        4.16.4   The Silent *r* 226

Appendix 229

Answers to Exercises 237

Notes 277

INTRODUCTION

English Start is intended for learners at the higher beginner's level. At this level the candidate is expected to have limited communication skills and should be expected to fulfill only practical needs that are simple and easy. Accuracy in the use of grammar in the present, past, simple, and continuous forms of the verb as well as limited use of the future tense is expected along with the proper use of nouns, adjectives, prepositions, pronouns, adverbs, and conjunctions. Fluency and style in language use are not expected.

The syllabus content has been organized around areas of themes, functions, and grammar, with the aim of arming students with the skills of speaking, writing, reading, and listening. It is by no means exhaustive. The choice of themes was based on the need to expose students to everyday events.

It is hoped that this text will also clear up many of the problem areas that are associated with English used by speakers of other languages, for example, "no is" and "can to." In this case, the negative form of the language is presented for practical use. Much confusion exists in the use of the pronouns and prepositions, and great effort has been made to clarify these points.

This book fully equips the candidate with the skills and knowledge needed to take on the challenges of the higher intermediate level.

Who Is *English Start* For?

English Language Students

The book is intended for use by students who are speakers of other languages and who wish to learn the language at the higher elementary level. Presented in a clear and simple format, this book will give English language students every opportunity to read, to write, to listen, and to speak the language. Correct grammatical use is strongly advised and is included to guide the student in the proper use of the language. In addition, tremendous emphasis is placed on the development of oral communication skills. Many people attempting to speak the language have all too often cut corners and have ended up communicating incorrectly. The book also offers techniques in pronunciation which will greatly assist the student. The work is also a wonderful guide to develop writing skills.

Teachers of English as a Foreign Language

The book is ideally suited for trainers. Topics are presented in a simple format with guidelines so that their tasks are simplified. It is intended for use by teachers as an aid to teaching, and numerous examples and grammatical exercises are provided to ensure that topics are fully covered. It assists teachers in encouraging students to speak. Situations that are relevant to the individual are presented, and great effort was made to include and highlight common problem areas.

Expected Results

The student should demonstrate pronunciation, intonation, and syntax acceptable to a native speaker in simple conversations on themes listed in the course as outlined in the table of contents. The student is expected to request and give information, to describe, locate, identify, and compare both orally and in writing. The student is also expected to acquire the skills of reading and listening comprehension.

Assessment of Competence

The assessment of the language is based on the following:

Oral Skills

Ability to communicate orally on simple topics or everyday events must be demonstrated. The appropriate stress here is on the use of vocabulary and the practical use of the language as well as accurate grammar and structure. Accurate grammar is important in spoken language. Fluency and style are skills that are only assessed at higher levels.

Writing Skills

Students are assessed on their ability to describe persons, places, and things; to compare, to identify, to locate, and to provide a simple account of events. Students should be familiar with grammar and should use it accurately when writing.

Reading Skills

Students are assessed on their ability to comprehend simple stories and articles pertaining to daily life and to world events by responding to questions.

Listening Skills

Students must be exposed to a native voice speaking on topics in the text. Students must demonstrate their ability to comprehend a native speaker by answering questions posed to them.

What Are the Specific Benefits of the Book?

The decision to compile an EFL book was made after careful consideration of the problems encountered in the delivery of EFL programs. In almost all cases, students and teachers alike rarely find one book that fulfills their need. Careful consideration was given to the provision of sufficient resource teaching material for trainers in the compilation of this book. The specific benefits of the book include the following:

1. *Relevant material.* The book contains real-life situations in all skill areas (i.e., reading, writing, speaking, and listening).

2. *Accepted standards and quality.* The book adopts internationally accepted standards and quality (See Pitman's Qualifications Spoken ESOL Guide. Publ City and Guilds Institute London 2000).

3. *Communication skills.* The book encourages oral communicative skills, which is what most students need. While it instructs in the language skills of reading, conversation, writing, and listening, much more emphasis was placed on encouraging oral skills through dialogue, role play, and conversation.

4. *Problem areas addressed.* The book deals directly with grammatical problems that are common to speakers of other languages (e.g., prepositions *can, to, for,* etc.).

5. *Clear and simple approach.* The book is presented in a clear and simple format. It seeks to encourage interest at all times.

6. *Specific audience.* The book is suitably designed for young students and for adults who need to quickly acquire practical language skills. With respect to the American market, the book is suitable for grade K–12 ESOL students at low intermediate level as determined by the Kansas Board of Education.

7. *Subject matter.* The book revolves around themes and functions. There are several themes from which different functions are demonstrated. Some main functions include the ability to describe, to request and give information, to locate, to identify, and to compare. The main objective is to enable the student to master the skills of reading, writing, listening, and speaking. While the use of grammar appears in the text as a skill, it is not considered a special skill. It is

an integral component of all aforementioned skills. Treatment of grammar is extensive at this level. Similarly, pronunciation appears as a skill in chapter 4 but is not regarded as a special skill.

To improve oral skills, special situations are presented for students to role play. This is an effort to expose students to real-life situations in the classroom. Another component of the oral skill is the student dialogue. This is a question-and-answer type dialogue which primarily serves to reinforce the accuracy of the grammar and to express ideas on some topics. The following subjects are presented:

CHAPTER 1	IDENTIFYING AND COMMUNICATING LOCATING ADRESSES DATES AND NUMBERS			
Skill	Function	Grammar	Theme	Verbs
Oral				
Conversation	Identifying oneself	Present and past tense	Personal	To be
		Simple and continuous tense	Identification	To do
				To have
		The interrogative	Greetings	
		How, when, where?	Introductions	
		Future tense	Meeting friends	Going to
		Negative *not*		Am not
		Noun and verb agreement	The staff	
			The group	
Dialogue	Locating	Prepositions	Places	
Q&A		in, on, at		
	Counting		Numbers	
			Cardinal	
			Ordinal	
			Dates	
Role play	Dealing with situations		Telephoning a friend	
			Arranging to meet	
Writing				
	Identifying	Present tense	Yourself	
			Age, address Nationality	
		Past tense	Identifying the things you did in the past week	

Listening				
	Comprehending a native speaker		Dates	
			Numbers	
			Places	
			"The Life of Sir Isaac Newton"	
Reading				
	Comprehending information Nonfiction		"Saving the Gorillas"	

CHAPTER 2	DESCRIBING COMPARING LOCATING			
Skill	Function	Grammar	Theme	Verbs
Oral				
Conversation	Describing	Pronouns	Telling me about	
		Adjectives	your family	
		Present tense	Personality and	
		Past tense	physical traits	
			Occupation	
			Activities	
			Age	To meet
		Who, whose		To read
		whom		To dine
				To eat
		Present tense of verb		To work
		Simple tense of verb		To enjoy
				To study
		Adjectives	The house	
		New		
	Comparing	Bigger		
Dialogue	Locating	Prepositions	The kitchen	
Q&A		Next to	Household items	
	Describing	That, which		
		Books, movies Music, food		
		Possessives		

		Mine, Yours		
		Reflexive		
		Myself		
		Homework		
Role play	Dealing with the situation		Renting a house	
			Having a party	

Skill	Function	Grammar	Theme	Verbs
Writing				
	Describing		A family activity	To celebrate
		Adverbs		
		More, most	Likes/dislikes	To like
			A movie	
	Advertising		Selling a house	
			Creating an ad	
Listening				
	Comprehending a native speaker		A wedding	
	Describing		Floor plans	
			Office, home	
Reading				
	Comprehending		Work begins at	to clean
	Suggestions		home	to cook
				to paint
	Fiction (Storytelling)		"The Boy from	
			Bogota"	
			"There Is a Mouse	
			in the House"	

CHAPTER 3	TIME & WEATHER EXPRESSING ABILITY/POLITENESS ADVERB CLAUSE OF TIME, CAUSE AND EFFECT			
Skill	**Function**	**Grammar**	**Theme**	**Verbs**
Oral				
Conversation	Describing		Time and weather	
		Nouns	Snow, clouds	
		Adjectives	Late, early	
			Hot	

Skill	Function	Grammar	Theme	Verbs
		Present, past		To get up
		Continuous	It is raining	To rain
		Simple	Hurry!	To be late
			You are late.	To awaken
	Comparing	Adjectives of comparison	Hotter, cooler	
	Expressing ability	Can, could		Can you turn the the air conditioning on?
				to stop, to leave
	Cause and effect	Because		We couldn't leave because of the rain
		Now that		
Dialogue	Expressing time	Prepositions	On time	
Q&A		At, in, on	At eight	
			At the moment	
	Expressing ability	Can, could	Can you?	To drive, To ski
Role play	Dealing with situations.		Accepting/ declining	To invite
			invitations	To accept
			Sorry, I can't.	To refuse
	Politeness		Can I help you?	
Writing				
	Describing	Adjectives	The weather	
		Adverbs	Very hot	
			A summer activity	

Skill	Function	Grammar	Theme	Verbs
Writing				
	Predicting	The Future tense	Predictions	To be
				will be
Listening				
	Comprehending a native speaker		Sun safety	To prevent
	Advising		Colds and flu	

Reading				
	Comprehending information non-fiction			"The Climate of Peru"	To change (seasons)
				"Is the Earth Getting Hotter?"	To rise

CHAPTER 4	GETTING AROUND: REQUESTING & GIVING INFORMATION LOCATING PEOPLE, THINGS, PLACES PREPOSITIONS: *NEXT TO, NEAR* ADJECTIVE CLAUSES: *WHEN, WHERE*			
Skill	**Function**	**Grammar**	**Theme**	**Verbs**
Oral				
Converse	Requesting and Giving Information	Present tense of the	Directions	To shop
		verb	To the bank	To buy
		How far?	To the shops	To sell
	Locating	Prepositions	Opposite	To find
			In front of	To get to
	Describing	Adjectives of description	Savings account	To change
				To open (an account)
	Comparing		Color, type	to cost
				to pay
		Adjectives of comparison	More expensive	To tell
				To need
				To fit
Dialogue	Describing	Prepositions	Getting there	
Q&A			By taxi,	
		When, where, as	Where do you	
		Adjective clauses	shop?	
Role play	Dealing with situations		Need to open	
			an account?	
			Looking for an	
			item?	
Writing				
	Describing		The neighborhood	
			City, town, restaurants	
Listening				
	Comprehending a native speaker	Future tense	"The Future of	To have, will have
			Communications"	To be, will be

Reading				
	Comprehending information Nonfiction	The Internet Reborn		
Pronunciation	Pronouncing		*ed* words *w* words *es* words	

CHAPTER 1

📖 **Identifying and Communicating**
📖 **Locating Addresses**
📖 **Dates and Numbers**

> **Skills Development**
> **Grammar & Exercises**
> **Nouns & Verbs**

1.0   Looking at the Parts of Speech: A Review

We begin with a look at the parts of speech. The parts of speech include nouns, verbs, pronouns, adjectives, adverbs, conjunctions, and prepositions. Look at the simple sentences below.

NOUN	PRONO	VERB	ADVERB	CONJUNC	PREPOSITI	ADJECTI
Tom the door		ran	quickly		to	
	He					
John television		is looking			at	new the
John Mary television		are looking		and	at	new the
	They					

Table 1: Types of Speech

Tom ran quickly to the door.

Tom is the noun because it is the name of a person.

Ran is the action word or verb.

Quickly modifies the verb and is the adverb. How did he run? Quickly.

To is the preposition. It shows the relationship between nouns and/or pronouns. Other prepositions are *at, in, on, for, by, with, of,* and *from.*

Door is a noun. It is the name of something.

John is watching the new television.

John and Mary are watching the new television.

And is a conjunction. It joins words. *Or, but,* and *nor* are other conjunctions.

New is the adjective. It describes the noun *television.*

Pronouns replace nouns in the sentence.

He is looking at the new television.

They are looking at the new television.

Hey! and *Oh!* are referred to as interjections.

Hey! Where are you going?

Oh! How lovely.

Exercise 1.0a Now identify the parts of speech in the following sentences by completing Table 2.

a.   Mary and I ran quickly to the bus.

b.   We saw the man running hurriedly from the house.

c.   Susan and I walked slowly to school.

d.   Tom and I always read the newspapers after dinner.

e.   Oh! You look wonderful.

f.   The house is a gray house.

g.   We are going to the beach.

h.   Mary is wearing a gray skirt.

i.   Anna is reading the newspaper.

j.   The book is on the table.

Table 2: Fill in the blanks

	Noun	Pronoun	Verb	Adverb	Conjunction	Preposition	Adjective
A.							
B.							
C.							
D.							
E.							
F.							
G.							
H.							
I.							
J.							

1.1   Looking at Nouns: A Review

1.   Types of nouns

Nouns can be divided into five groups.(Nesfield's English Grammar, republished; Caribbean Educational Publishers, 1998)

   a.   **The proper noun**; for example, *Mary, China*. The capital letter is used all the time.

   b.   **The common noun**; for example, *book, student, children*

   c.   **The collective noun**; for example, *herds* of animals

   d.   **The material noun**; for example, *soil, grass, water*

   e.   **The abstract noun**; for example, *truth, poverty, honesty, kindness*[3]

2.   Gender of nouns—Masculine/feminine/neuter

Nouns are masculine or feminine depending on its sex (i.e., male or female). An example of a neuter gender would be *student* which can be either male or female. A neuter form is neither male nor female (e.g., *rock*).

3.   Forming the plural nouns

The plural can be formed by adding *-s* to the singular, as in *cow* to *cows* or by adding *-es,* as in *dish* to *dishes*. Plurals can also be formed by changing an ending *y* to *-ies* as in *baby* to *babies*, and by a change in the singular *-ief* to *-ves*, such as *thief* to *thieves*. Some nouns have no plural forms (*sheep, fish, information*) and some have no singular forms (*news, scissors, thanks*).

4.   Adding the apostrophe (')

To determine possession, the apostrophe *-'s* is used (e.g. *Mary's* house, a *man's* world).

To determine the plural possessive, the apostrophe is added after the word (e.g., *sons'*).

In cases where the noun changes form as in man to men, the apostrophe is added as in *men's*.

Exercise 1.1a Form the plural of the following nouns.

Book _____   Cousin_____   Shoe_____

Enemy_____	Wife_____	Friend_____
Thief_____	Loaf_____	Shop_____
Day_____	Cook_____	Man_____
Dish_____	Woman_____	Fish_____
Child_____	Grocery_____	Foot_____

Exercise 1.1b Change the sentences by using the apostrophe.

Example: The pen of the girl

The girl's pen

a. The bag of the lady

_____

b. The car of the man

_____

c. The room for ladies

_____

d. The washroom for men

_____

e. The milk of all the cows

_____

Exercise 1.1c Identify the noun and type of noun (proper, common, collective, material, abstract) in the sentences below.

a. Susan is going to the party.

b. Fish live in water.

c. The students are walking around the school.

d. Poverty is a crime.

e. China is a big country.

f. The food is good.

g.   The group of lions is in the bush. (The collective noun is singular, agreeing with *is*.)

h.   The family is small.

i.   People are nice.

j.   The soil is dry.

k.   New York is a big city.

Exercise 1.1d Practice using nouns by making simple sentences. Include the following:

A proper noun

_____

A common noun

_____

A material noun

_____

A collective noun

_____

An abstract noun

_____

1.2   Conjunctions *And, But,* or *Nor:* A Review

Conjunctions connect words or phrases. Look at the examples below:

Mary and Tessa are going to school.

The table and chair are old.

The furniture is old but expensive.

You can take a bus or a train.

The conjunction *or* is often used with *either. Neither/nor* and *either/or* are paired conjunctions.

You can either take a bus or a train.

You can either watch TV or listen to the radio.

Neither Mary nor Jane is at home.

Exercise 1.2a Fill in the blanks with the conjunctions *and, but, or,* and, *nor.*

a.   Tom _____ Andy are leaving for school. Neither Tom _____ Andy did his homework.

b.   The pair of shoes is old _____ comfortable.

c.   Either do your homework_____ wash the dishes.

d.   Both Marissa _____ Laurie are going to the show.

e.   The game is on at four o'clock. You can watch it here _____ at your house.

f.   My dress is red _____ blue.

g.   The water looks clean _____ it is dirty.

h.   Either John _____ Paul is going to the conference.

i.   Either John _____ Paul left his car here.

j.   Both Lisa _____ Cindy are tired.

Exercise 1.2b Now combine the following using the conjunctions *and, but, nor,* and *or.*

Mary likes coffee. She does not like milk.

_____

Jenny is not going to the party. Neither is Cindy.

_____

Mary likes clothes. Mary likes shoes.

_____

You can watch cable TV. You can read a good book.

_____

Kate likes swimming. She does not like music.

_____

1.3   *A, An, The*: A Review

A and *an* are indefinite articles. *The* is the definite article.

Let's look at some examples:

> *A* young girl came to see you. (This means any young girl. *A* shows that the girl is indefinite.)

> *The* young girl came to see you. (This means a specific young girl. *The* shows that the girl is definite.)

> *An* owl is a bird.

An is used before *a, e, i,o, u* vowels.

A and *an* are used with the singular. *The* is used with the singular and the plural.

Exercise 1.3a Fill in the blanks with the correct article.

a.   It is _____old house.

b.   _____books are on the table.

c.   It is_____ interesting story.

d.   It is _____ empty house.

e.   _____ people are in the room.

f.   It takes _____ hour to get to work.

g.   Mary wants _____new dress.

h.   The new shop is _____mile away.

i.   _____ shops are open today.

j.   May I have _____ apple?

Exercise 1.3b Practice the definite and indefinite articles by making simple sentences using the nouns below:

keys, car, umbrella, computers

1._____	2._____
3._____	4._____

1.4   Looking at Verbs: Present and Past Tense

The sentences compare the past and present tense of the verb—go.

I go to school.   I went to school.

Let us look further at the verbs *to have, to do, to be,* and *to go*—present and past tense.

The present tense describes an action that takes place currently. The past tense describes an action that has already happened. Verbs are action words.

Table 3: The present and past tense of *to be, to do, to have,* and *to go*

Present	Past	Present	Past
To Be		To Have	
I am	I was	I have	I had
He/she is	He/she/was	You have	You had
You are	You were	He/She has	You had
It is	It was	It has	It had
We are	We were	We have	We had
You are	You were	You have	You had
They are	They were	They have	They had
To Do		To Go	
I do	I did	I go	I went
He/ She does	He/She did	You go	You went
You do	You did	He/She goes	He/She went
It does	It did	It goes	It went
We do	We did	We go	We went
You do	You did	You go	You went
They do	They did	They go	They went

These are commonly used verbs, and you need to know them. Look at the simple sentences.

Present	Past
a. I have a dog.	I had a dog.
b. I am tired.	I was tired.
c. I go to school by bus.	I went to school by bus.
d. I do my work everyday.	I did my homework yesterday.

Now let's look at some examples of questions and answers.

Questions	Answers	Present Simple	Past Simple
a. Are you tired?	Yes I am.	✓	
b. Were you tired?	Yes I was.		✓
c. How are you?	I am tired.	✓	
d. Where did they go?	They went to the shop.		✓
e. Has he any money?	Yes, he has money.	✓	

Exercise 1.4a Let's practice the present simple. Fill in the blanks.

a.   She _____ to the shop every day. (to go)

b.   They _____ three cars. (to have)

c.   He_____hungry. (to be)

d.   We _____fast food. (to like)

e.   He_____English every day. (to study)

f.   I _____ to the gym. (to go)

g.   They _____ late. (to be)

h.   We _____ sleepy. (to be)

i.   I_____ a good job. (to have)

j.   She _____ magazines. (to have)

Exercise 1.4b Let's practice the past simple. Fill in the blanks.

a.   I_____to church on Sunday. (to go)

b.   They _____ a big party. (to have)

c.   We_____the show. (to like)

d.   She _____on the phone. (to be)

e.   He _____his homework. (to do)

f. They _____ to Texas. (to go)

g. I _____ tired. (to be)

h. My father _____ a big house. (to have)

i. Maria _____ the new dress. (to like)

j. My mother _____ the shopping. (to do)

1.5   The Present and Past Continuous *-ing* Endings

The continuous forms are actions that are not complete but are continuous.
Let's look at the examples. The continuous form uses the verb *to be* plus the
action verb.

Present Continuous	Past Continuous
a. I am walking my dog.	I was walking my dog.
b. He is having lunch.	He was having lunch.
c. He is eating.	He was eating.
d. He is doing the washing.	He was doing the washing.

He is watching TV.

He is listening to the radio.

The present continuous can also be used to express the future.

Let's look at some examples using the verbs *to go, to come,* and *to have.*

Examples:

Future

- I am going on vacation next week.

- They are coming to dinner tonight.

- We are going to the show later.

- They are having fish for dinner.

Exercise 1.5a Let's practice the continuous form of the present tense. Fill in the blanks.

a.   I _____ home. (to go)

b.   He _____ to the man. (to talk)

c.   We _____ at the door. (to stand)

d.   She _____ with her sister. (to sit)

e.   They _____ for her. (to wait)

f.   Anna _____ her hair. (to comb)

g.   Susan _____ her house. (to clean)

h.   Pablo _____ the game. (to watch)

i.   Antonio _____his car. (to drive)

j.   The animals _____ grass. (to eat)

Now let's look at examples of the past continuous.

Examples:

- She was walking the dog yesterday when the rain started.

- Sylvia was cooking dinner when the doorbell rang.

- They were doing the painting when the ladder fell.

- He was having dinner at the time.

– They were going to the show when the car broke down.

Exercise 1.5b Practice the past continuous by filling in the blanks.

a. I _____ when the phone rang. (to sleep)

b. He _____ to the lady when the doorbell rang. (to talk)

c. She _____ home at the time of the accident. (to go)

d. They _____ along the pavement when he fell. (to walk)

e. He _____ his car when it began to rain. (to drive)

f. We _____ our homework when the lights went out. (to do)

g. They_____at television when they heard a knock on the door. (to look)

h. I _____ when the guests arrived. (to cook)

i. She _____ at the time. (to study)

j. He _____ for her when the phone rang. (to wait)

Exercise 1.5c Fill in the blanks with the past tense.

a. Yesterday I _____ to school. (to go)

b. Last night we_____ to the cinema. (to go) We_____ the show. (to like)

c. I _____ my homework last night. (to do)

d. Yesterday I _____ fish for dinner. (to have)

e. They _____ a big house. (to have)

f. We _____ tired after the long journey. (to be)

g. He _____ his father after many years. (to see)

h. I _____ happy for him. He passed his exam. (to be)

i. He _____ all the work. (to do)

j. They _____ him at the shop. (to see)

1.6   Using the Irregular Verbs

Let's look at the present and past forms of some irregular verbs.

Table 4: Past and present forms of the irregular verbs

Present	Past		Present	Past
buy	bought		feel	felt
drive	drove		sit	sat
forget	forgot		sleep	slept
become	became		hear	heard
know	knew		think	thought
drink	drank		eat	ate
choose	chose		sell	sold
be	was/were		speak	spoke
give	gave		come	came
run	ran		begin	began
swim	swam		write	wrote
see	saw		think	thought
do	did		teach	taught
sleep	slept		read	read

Let's compare the tenses.

Present	Past
We swim in the ocean.	We swam in the ocean.
They sleep all day.	They slept all day.
We buy lots of clothes.	We bought lots of clothes.
We speak to him.	We spoke to him.
Present continuous	**Past continuous**
We are swimming in the ocean.	We were swimming in the ocean.
They are sleeping all day.	They were sleeping all day.
We are buying lots of clothes.	We were buying lots of clothes.
We are speaking to him.	We were speaking to him.

Exercise 1.6a Practice the past tense of the irregular verbs by filling in the blanks.

a. She _____to close the door. (to forget)

b. They _____classes on Saturday. (to begin)

c. We _____the loud bang. (to hear)

d. I _____ for miles yesterday. (to drive)

e. Sandra _____tired. (to feel)

f. He _____ all the food. (to eat)

g. We _____ everything. (to sell)

h. She _____ the robber. (to see)

i. Anna _____a new car. (to buy)

j. I _____ my aunt a letter. (to write)

Exercise 1.6b Fill in the blanks with present continuous of the irregular verbs.

a. I _____ at my friend's house. (to sleep)

b. We _____ a new house. (to buy)

c. She _____ a letter to her friend in England.(to write)

d. They _____clothes. (to sell)

e. Marta _____ to him. (to speak)

f. Fiona _____a dress. (to choose)

g He _____ home. (to run)

h. We _____ about it. (to think)

i. Alicia _____ lunch. (to eat)

j. We _____ to work. (to drive)

Exercise 1.6c Fill in the blanks with the past continuous of the irregular verbs.

a. We _____ about him when he walked in. (to speak)

b. He _____ at the time the lights went off. (to eat)

c. She _____ at her desk when the phone rang. (to sit)

d. They _____ to work when the rain started. (to begin)

e. They _____ the newspapers when the bus came. (to read)

f. Anita _____ something at the mall when the man appeared. (to buy)

g. Tony _____ to the bank when he fell. (to go)

h. I _____ on the chair when it broke. (to sit)

i. I _____ home at the time. (to drive)

j. He _____ her to swim when the bell rang. (to teach)

1.7   The *-ed* Verbs

The past tense is formed by adding *-ed* to the verb.

Table 5: Past and present forms of the *-ed* verbs

Verb	Past Tense
like	liked
live	lived
walk	walked
smile	smiled
jump	jumped
cook	cooked
watch	watched
wait	waited
talk	talked
listen	listened

Verb	Past Tense
stop	stopped
rest	rested
return	returned
study	studied
rain	rained
try	tried
reply	replied
open	opened
start	started
enjoy	enjoyed

Let's compare the tenses again.

Present	Past
He smiles happily.	He smiled happily.
We watch movies.	We watched movies.
We cook dinner every night.	We cooked dinner last night.
We wait for her.	We waited for her.
We talk all day.	We talked all day.
They walk to school.	They walked to school.
Present continuous	**Past continuous**
He is smiling happily.	He was smiling happily.
We are watching a movie.	We were watching a movie.
We are waiting for her.	We were waiting for her.
We are talking all day.	We were talking all day.
They are walking to school.	They were walking to school.

Practice the verbs by adding *-ing* and *-ed* endings.

1. Add *-ing* to the verbs.

    go   _____   dry   _____

    sleep   _____   sit   _____

    begin   _____   leave   _____

    run   _____   come   _____

    enjoy   _____   die   _____

    fry   _____   eat   _____

    stop   _____   sell   _____

    hide   _____   write   _____

2. Add *-ed* to the verbs.

    dry   _____   fry   _____

    hope   _____   visit   _____

    bore   _____   dance   _____

    die   _____   help   _____

    try   _____   stay   _____

    snow   _____   plan   _____

    cry   _____   rest   _____

    need   _____   want   _____

    believe   _____   count   _____

    call   _____   shout   _____

Exercise 1.7a Write sentences using the verbs below.

to walk   to study   to cook   to clean

a. In the past tense

b. In the past continuous

Exercise 1.7b Write sentences using the irregular verbs below.

| to speak | to sit | to go | to come | to sleep |

a. In the past tense

b. In the past continuous

Exercise 1.7c Fill in the blanks using the words below.

| drove | stopped | ate | took | rested | returned |

Last weekend, we _____ a long trip to the countryside. We _____ for four hours. Then we _____ at a beach near the coast and had lunch. The food was tasty and we _____ a lot. After lunch, we _____ for a while and much later we _____ home.

Exercise 1.7d Complete the sentences using the past simple and past continuous tenses of the verbs in parentheses.

1). I (to hear) _____ a bang outside my house last night. I (to sleep) _____ at the time. It (to wake) _____ me up.

2). Last night I (to visit) _____ my friend at his home. At the time, he (to read) _____ a book. He (to stop) _____ reading, and (to speak) _____ to me.

3). On Sundays we always have a big lunch. Last Sunday we (to cook) _____ chicken. While we (to eat) _____, my aunt (to arrive) _____. She (to bring) _____ a chocolate cake for dessert.

4). My brother (to have) _____ an accident. While he (to drive) _____ his car, a man (to run) _____ across the road. My brother braked suddenly, and his car (to skid) _____ off the road.

5). I (to walk) _____ home from school when the rain (to start) _____ to fall. I (to take) _____ shelter under a tree.

6). Last summer we (to go) _____ to Florida for our vacation. We (to see) _____ many wonderful places and we (to eat) _____ in many good restaurants. We (to stay) _____ for one week.

7). While she (to dress) _____for work, the telephone (to ring) _____. She quickly (to answer) _____it.

8). I (to study) _____ at the university for three years before (to start) _____my first job. I (to work) _____at a factory. I (to be) _____ the manager.

9). Last night I (to do) _____ my homework. While I (to do) _____my homework, my sister (to come) _____ home.

10). Last night we (to dance) _____ all night. It (to be) _____ great fun. We _____ (to arrive) home at two o'clock in the morning.

1.8   The Active *-ing* and Passive *-ed* Forms

1. *The present continuous.* Look at the examples below.

    He is painting the house. (active)

    The house is being painted by him. (passive)

Exercise 1.8a. Convert the following active forms to the passive:

a.   The factory in Germany is making wine.

    _____

b.   The history class is boring them.

    _____

c.   The gym exercises are tiring him.

    _____

d.   He is cleaning the garden.

    _____

e.   He is trimming the plants.

    _____

2. *The past continuous.* Look at the examples below.

    The English class was boring them. (active)

    The students were bored by the English class. (passive)

Exercise 1.8b. Convert the following active past continuous verbs to passive past continuous:

a.   The walk to the village was tiring them.   _____

b.   The morning air was refreshing them.   _____

c.   The man's singing was irritating her.   _____

d.   The woman was getting angry because of the traffic.   _____

e.   The show was amusing them.   _____

-ed verbs:

angry-angered; refresh-refreshed; irritate-irritated; tire-tired; amuse-amused

> Note: Verbs such as *to like, to need, to want, to believe,* and *to know* are not used in the continuous form.

1.9   Using the Negative: *Not*

Let's look at the verbs *to be* and *to do* in the negative form.

Table 6: The negative form, past and present, of the verbs *to be* and *to do*

Present	Past	Present	Past
To Be		To Do	
I am not	1 was not	I do not	I did not
You are not	You were not	You do not	You did not
He/she is not	He/she were not	He/she does not	He/she did not
It is not	It was not	It does not	It did not
We are not	We were not	We do not	We did not
They are not	They were not	They do not	They did not

Note for Spanish speakers: *No es* is translated *it is not*. not *no is*

Sentence	Abbreviated Form
I am not going to school.	I'm not going to school.
I did not go to school.	I didn't go to school.
I do not like vegetables.	I don't like vegetables.
We do not like noise.	We don't like noise.
We did not like the show.	We didn't like the show.
They do not like her.	They don't like her.
They did not like her.	They didn't like her.
Is it not great?	Isn't it great?
Are you not going?	Aren't you going?
He was not happy.	He wasn't happy.
They were not happy.	They weren't happy.
He has no money.	He hasn't any money.
He had no money.	He hadn't any money.

Exercise 1.9a Answer the following in complete sentences using the negative.

a. Did you go to the party?   _____

b. Are you going to the shop?   _____

c. Have you seen Ann?   _____

d. Have you finished your homework? _____

e. Did you like the math class?   _____

f. Do you like pizza?   _____

g. Did you feed the dog?   _____

h. Are you hungry?   _____

i. Were you sleepy?   _____

j. Is the movie good?   _____

k. Were you tired?   _____

l. Did he go to Spain?   _____

Exercise 1.9b Complete the following sentences with the verbs in the negative past tense.

a. I (to like) _____ the party. The people (to be) _____ very nice, but the food was bad.

b. We (to go) _____ to the wedding. It was too far to travel.

c. Andy (to wash) _____ his clothes.

d. They (to enjoy) _____ the movie.

e. She (to be) _____ happy with her new school.

f. I (to cook) _____ dinner.

g. They (to walk) _____ home. They took a bus.

h. He (to pass) _____ his exams.

i. She (to spend) _____ any money.

j. We (to shop) _____ at the malls.

1.10   Noun and Verb Agreement

1.10.1   Singular and Plural

The general rule is that singular nouns and pronouns agree with singular verbs; the same rule applies to the plural. Look at the examples below.

1.   is, are, was, were

is	was
The book is on the table.	The book was on the table.

are	were
The books are on the table.	The books were on the table.

2.   has, have, had

has	have
My friend has my books.	My friends have my books.

had	
My friend had my books.	My friends had my books.

3.   sell, sold, lives, lived

sell	lives
The shop sells many things.	She lives in New York.
The shops sell many things.	They live in New York.

sold	lived
The shop sold many things.	She lived in New York.
The shops sold many things.	They lived in New York.

Exercise 1.10a Fill in the blanks using the present tense of the verbs in parentheses.

a.   Mary _____ all day. (to sleep)

b.   She _____ cakes at the mall. (to sell)

c. The students _____ no classes. (to have)

d. I _____ no shoes. (to have)

e. They _____ many things at the market. (to buy)

f. He _____ a lot of clothes. (to buy)

g. We _____ looking at the game. (to be)

h. Anna _____ wearing a new dress. (to be)

i. She _____ all day. (to eat)

j. They _____ all day. (to eat)

Exercise 1.10b Fill in the blanks with the past tense.

a. My grandfather _____ a house in Colombia. He _____ in Colombia. (to have, to live)

b. My father and mother _____ Peru. (to visit)

c. He _____ many houses. (to have)

d. They _____ a lot of money. (to have)

e. She _____ cakes at the shop. (to sell)

f. They _____ cars at the factory. (to sell)

g. She _____ her clothes at the mall. (to buy)

h. They _____ their clothes at the mall. (to buy)

i. I _____ a new car. (to have)

j. We _____ the food. (to like)

1.10.2   The Irregular Cases

1.   Using Non-countable Nouns

Non-countable nouns are singular.

Let's look at the examples below.

Work music rain water snow information money furniture weather

_____

_____

_____

_____

_____

2.   Time and Distance

Five hours is a long time to get there!	Five hours was a long time to get there!
It is one thousand miles away.	It was one thousand miles away.

3.   Collective Nouns

Collective nouns are singular.

_____

_____

Now consider the use of the verb when the pronouns are used. The verb is plural.

My family is loving and caring.	They are wonderful.
The staff is having lunch.	They are having lunch.
The group is tired.	They are tired.
The team is playing a game.	They are playing a game.

4.   Using *each, either, neither, everyone*

These require the use of the singular.

Each	either
Each of the students is going on the trip.	Either Tom or Anna is going on the trip.
Neither	**everyone**
Neither Tom nor Anna is going on the trip.	Everyone is going on the trip.

Exercise 1.10c Complete the following sentences. Use the present tense of the verb *to be: is* or *are*.

a.   My family _____ going shopping. They _____ going shopping.

b.   The football team _____ playing on Sunday. They _____ playing on Sunday.

c.   The group of lions is sleeping. They _____ sleeping.

d.   My family _____ small. It is made up of four persons.

e.   The group _____ small. It is made up of five persons.

f.   Ten miles _____ a long distance to walk.

g.   Six hours _____ a long wait for the flight to Paris.

h.   There _____ a lot of rain today.

i.   There _____ much money in the banks.

j.   There _____ many people here.

Note: *Much* is used with non-countable nouns; *many* with countable nouns.

Exercise 1.10d Fill in the blanks using the past tense of the verbs *to be: was* or *were*.

a.   There _____ no money in the bank.

b.   Yesterday there _____ a lot of work to do.

c. There _____a lot of rain yesterday.

d. There _____ no information on the subject matter.

e. There _____ a lot of people at the mall.

f. There _____few computers at the school.

g. There _____much noise at the mall.

h. There _____many students at school.

i. There_____ much rain yesterday.

j. There_____ no water in the taps.

Skills Development
Grammar & Exercise
Questions Words

The question words: *What? Who? Whom? Where? Whose? Which? How? Why? When?*

1.11 The Interrogative Forms

a.   The interrogative adjectives

Which?	What?
Which computer is your computer?	What type of book is it?

This?	
Is this book your book?	

b.   The interrogative adverbs.

How?	When?
How are you?	When are you coming back?
Where?	Why
Where are you going?	Why are you leaving?

c.   The interrogative pronouns.

Who?	Whom?
Who are you?	Whom is it for?
Whose?	Which?
Whose house is it?	Which is it?

Now let's continue with question-and-answer sentences.

Exercise 1.11a Supply the questions. Use the present tense

a.   _____? I am fine, thank you.

b. _____? I am going for a walk.

c. _____? I am cooking dinner.

d. _____? The pen is my pen.

e. _____? I live in America.

f. _____? I am studying English because I want to travel.

g. _____? I am twelve years old.

h. _____? I am going to the doctor.

i. _____? I am coming home at ten o'clock.

j. _____? I am studying English.

Exercise 1.11b Now supply questions using the past tense.

a. _____? I went to the doctor.

b. _____? I read a book on Sunday.

c. _____? It was Anna's book

d. _____? They lived in Spain.

e. _____? She was speaking to her mother.

f. _____? She was my best friend.

g. _____? He was five years old then.

h. _____? The house was my house.

i. _____? My exam was on Monday.

j. _____? I was sad about my dog.

Exercise 1.11c . Supply the questions and answers. Complete the following:

QUESTION	ANSWER
	I graduated in 1999.
	■
	I started working in 2000.
	I am an accountant.
How old were you when you started high school?	
	My hobby is reading.
Where did you study English?	
Which university did you attend?	
Who do you live with?	
	My favorite color is green.
	My favorite food is Italian food.

Note: We often use the interrogative forms when we identify ourselves and when we greet and meet people.

PERSONAL IDENTIFICATION

IT'S IMPORTANT!

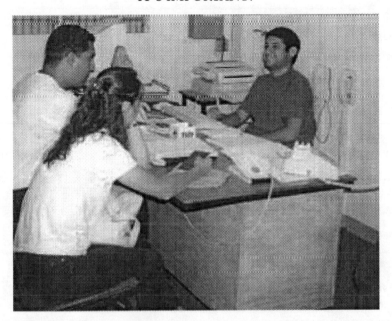

It is important to have identification, also known as ID. In today's world, people have cards that carry their name and identification numbers. Personal identification is part of everyday life.

Now, let's look at something more personal. It is an interview, and the person is giving information about herself.

AT AN INTERVIEW

Skills Development Requesting and Giving Information

1.12   Conversation 1. Personal Identification

Practice the interview with a friend or classmate. Fill in the blanks with the information pertaining to you.

Q. How are you?

A._____

Q. What is your name?

A. _____

Q. What is your nationality?

A. _____

Q. What is your date of birth?

A. _____

Q. What do you do?

A_____

Q. What is your marital status?

A_____

Q. How many brothers and sisters do you have?

A. _____

Q. Where do you live?

A. _____

Q. What is your telephone number?

A. _____

Q. How old are you?

A_____

Now repeat the questions above to your classmate.

GREETINGS!

Skills Development
Oral Skills
Conversation

1.13   Conversation 2. Greeting and Introducing

Communicating with people is very important. We can form links and make new friends.

Practice the following conversations with a friend or classmate.

1. Greeting and introducing yourself

–   Hello, my name is Juan. What is your name?

–   My name is Anna. I am a student.

–   What are you studying, Anna?

–   I am studying English.

–   That's wonderful, Anna. Where do you live?

–   I live in Valencia on Rose Avenue at # 10.

2. Introducing someone

–   Hello. How are you?

– Fine, thank you. I would like you to meet my father.

– Glad to meet you, Mr. Lopez. Do sit down. What would you like to drink? Coffee?

– Thank you. Coffee would be fine.

"Coffee would be fine."

ON THE PHONE

3.

a) Greeting someone by phone (formal)

R r r r r r

– Can I speak with Mr. Brown, please?

– May I ask who is calling?

– Yes, tell him it's Mr. Thomas.

– Yes, of course. One moment, please.

b) Greeting someone by phone (informal)

R r r r r r r

– Hello?

– Hello, Consuelo, how are you?

– Fine. And you?

– Great. Let's meet for lunch.

– OK. What time?

– Twelve O'clock.

– Where?

– At the mall.

– Fine, see you there. Bye.

– Bye.

4. Greeting a stranger

– Excuse me, please.

– Yes? Can I help you?

– Yes. Is this the bus to the city?

– No. The bus to the city is number twenty. It passes here every hour. You just need to wait.

– Thank you very much.

1.14   Conversation 3. Meeting Friends

Practice the following conversations with a friend or classmate.

Situation 1.

You meet your English-speaking friend on the street. Greet him and find out what he is doing.

—   Hello. How are you? Where are you going?

—   I am going to the Internet cafe. Where are you going?

—   I am going shopping. By the way what are you doing later?

—   Nothing. Why?

—   Maybe we can meet at the disco.

—   That would be fine. When are you going to be there? What time?

—   I am getting there at 10:00 PM.

—   Great. Bye then. See you later.

—   Bye.

Situation 2.

You meet your English-speaking friend at the mall. He looks unhappy. Find out what the problem is.

—   Hi. How are you? Are you okay?

—   No, I am not. I feel terrible.

—   Why? What's wrong?

- I lost my wallet.

- Oh no! Where did you lose it?

- I don't know. It's awful. I lost all my money.

- Don't worry. Let's go and look for it. Maybe we can still find it.

Situation 3.

You are at a staff Christmas party, and you wish to introduce your companion. What do you say?

- Hi. How are you? Great party.

- Yes. The entire staff is here. Everyone is having a wonderful time.

- This is my friend Lisa.

- Hi, Lisa. Nice to meet you.

- Wonderful to meet you too.

- Let's get something to drink.

- Yes, let's.

Skills Development
Oral Skills
Role Plays

1.15   Role Play: Dealing with the Situation

a. Eloisa meets her English-speaking friends at the disco. She wants to introduce her friend Antonio to them. What does she say?

b. Introduce your classmate to another person.

c. Your friend from Ireland is visiting you. Introduce him/her to your parents. Find out where he/she wants to go and what he/she wants to do. How long is she staying?

d. You are at the office. The phone rings. Answer it and find out what the person wants.

e. You are in an English-speaking country. You need a taxi. Greet a stranger and ask for help.

f. Make a simple arrangement by phone to meet your friend for lunch.

g. You are at a restaurant, and you don't understand the menu. Ask for help.

h. Call a friend and ask him or her to meet you at the disco.

i. You are supposed to meet some people at ten o'clock. Call and say you can't make it.

j. The immigration officer at the airport asks you for your address and nationality. Tell him.

1.16   Days of the Week, Months of Year, Numbers, Addresses

Some useful vocabulary:

Birthday
Day
Daily
Date
Birth
Death
Holiday
Month
Monthly
Year
Yearly
Week
Weekly
Weekend
Anniversary

Let's look at the days of the week and the months of the year.

Table 7: Days of the week and months the year:

Months	Days
January	Monday
February	Tuesday
March	Wednesday
April	Thursday
May	Friday
June	Saturday
July	Sunday
August	
September	
October	
November	
December	

a.   Can you write dates?

What is the date today?

_____

What was the date yesterday?

_____

What will be the date tomorrow?

_____

When is your birthday?

_____

Give the dates of three national holidays.

_____

b.   Can you count?

NUMBERS 1–110

10	Ten
20	Twenty
25	Twenty-five
30	Thirty
34	Thirty-four
40	Forty
50	Fifty
58	Fifty-eight
60	Sixty
61	Sixty-one
70	Seventy
80	Eighty
90	Ninety
93	Ninety-three
100	One hundred
101	One hundred and one
109	One hundred and nine
110	One hundred and ten

Now practice counting.

Count from 10–20, 21–35, 81–105

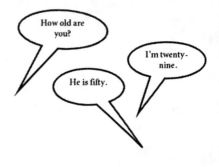

Skills Development Grammar& Exercises Locating

1.17   Using Prepositions: Locating Places and Dates

Table 8: A demonstration of the use of prepositions

IN	ON	AT
a country	a river	a party
a city	a boat	# 5 Alberto St
a state	a ship	home
a province	a plane	Time; e.g. at 8.00AM
a county	a train	weekends
a room	a street	the moment
a car	the coast	a place
the year	days	
the month		
a building		

Let's look at some examples.

He is <u>on</u> a plane.   She is sitting <u>at</u> her desk

She goes shopping <u>on</u> Fridays   They live <u>in</u> the city

Exercise 1.17a Look at the sentences below. Fill in the blanks with a suitable preposition: *in, at,* or *on.*

a.   She was looking _____ television last night.

b.   He was _____ the computer when the phone rang.

c.   I was _____ bed reading my book when the doorbell rang.

d.   He was _____ the phone for a long time.

e.   Maria was sitting _____ her desk.

f.   _____ Sundays we go to church.

g. She lives_____ France.

h. My mother is _____ home.

i. He sleeps_____a boat.

j. She is _____ the classroom.

Let's look at some more examples.

She lives on Rose Avenue.	They lived in Caracas.
She lived at #4 Rose Avenue.	He lives in an apartment.
She was born in 1986.	I was born on the tenth of May.

Exercise 1.17b

Fill in the blanks with a suitable preposition.

a. Graciela lives_____the country of Brazil_____the city of Rio de Janiero.

b. He lives _____ Avenida Brasilia _____20 Calle de Playa.

c. I live _____the country of Venezuela _____the city of Caracas _____ Avenida de Rio _____30 Calle de Sucre.

d. My house is very big. It is situated_____5 Alberto Street _____ the city of Madrid _____ Viewmont Avenue.

e. We are Americans. We live_____the East Coast of the United States.

f. My mother is _____ home, cooking dinner.

g. Alma and Graciela are _____home. Usually _____ 9.00AM they are _____ school.

h. There are many things _____ the house. We live _____ a big house.

i. Marta was born _____Sunday _____the month of April _____ the year 1989.

j   They live _____ the West Coast.

Skills Development
Oral Skills
Q&A

1.18   Student Dialogue

Let's practice using prepositions.

Ask your classmate a simple question. Write the answers down.

Student	a	I am looking for the dictionary. Do you know where it is?
Student	b	
Student	a	Where is the teacher?
Student	b	
Student	a	Where is your English book?
Student	b	
Student	a	Where do you have lunch? Dinner?
Student	b	
Student	a	Do you do work at home on the computer?
Student	b	
Student	a	Do you live in the city?
Student	b	
Student	a	What country do you live in?
Student	b	
Student	a	What is your home address?
Student	b	

Student	a	What is your office address?
Student	b	
Student	a	What age did you begin school?
Student	b	

Find the answers to these simple questions.

a. How many students are in your school?

b. What is your telephone number?

c. Do you watch the news on TV?

d. What is your father's age?

e. What do you do on Sundays?

f. Give the date of one national holiday.

g. What is the human population of your country?

h. Would you prefer to vacation on a cruise ship or to stay at a beach resort?

i. Do you stay at home a lot?

j. Do you talk on the phone a lot?

Skills Development
Listen and Speak

1.19   Script 1. Dates, Places, and Numbers.

Someone is needed to read Script 1. Listen to the speaker and repeat the sentences.

1. I was born in the month of May in the year 1989.

2. I was born on the tenth of May 1989.

3. Christmas day is the twenty-fifth of December. I was born on Christmas day.

4. I am twelve years old. I was born on the sixth of March in the year 1992.

5. My sister's birthday is on the third of June.

6. Trends Boutique is on Fifth Avenue in New City.

7. He is twenty-six years old.

8. He was born in nineteen seventy-eight (1978).

9. My grandmother is eighty-five.

10. She was born in 1919.

11. She lives in an apartment.

12. They live on Alberto Street.

13. They live at 25 Alberto Street.

14. She is sitting at her desk.

15. They live in the city. She lives on the West Coast.

16. At the moment, she is on the phone.

1.20   Script 2. The Life of Sir Isaac Newton

Someone is needed to read Script 2 (appendix 1). Listen to the speaker and answer the questions below.

1.   What is the nationality of the famous scientist Sir Isaac Newton?

2.   In what year was he born?

3.   When did his father die?

4.   At what age did he become a professor?

5.   What is the date of his death?

6.   Where did he die?

Skills Development
Grammar & Exercises
Nouns & Verbs

1.21　Reading Comprehension: Save the Gorillas

The World Wildlife Fund for Nature

Source:www.worldwildlife.org

Let's read.

WWF and Gorillas

The World Wide Fund for Nature—also known as The World Wildlife Fund (WWF) in the United States and Canada—is an international conservation organization dedicated to the protection of wildlife. According to the WWF, "the largest of the great apes, the gorilla, is among our most endangered species. Having faced decades of civil war in the region, gorillas are now threatened by the occurrence of habitat loss, poaching for the bushmeat trade, and the spread of dangerous diseases like Ebola.

While the efforts to safeguard the different subspecies are meeting with different levels of success, protecting all the animals remains the most important thing for WWF. Almost totally destroyed, the mountain gorilla population, which still numbers under 700 individuals, is now beginning to show an increase, thanks to a dedicated effort of the WWF. But the western lowland gorilla, the most numerous and widespread of the four subspecies, faces a severe Ebola crisis which, recent reports show, has caused a 56 percent decline in population across its range, with some of the hardest hit areas suffering even more.

WWF continues to work in the field in order to address these threats and protect these wondrous and endangered animals, hoping to provide a more secure future for the gorilla.

Source: www.worldwildlife.org.

1. What threatens the life of the gorillas?

2. What is the population of the mountain gorillas?

3. What is the major threat to the western lowland gorilla?

4. Are gorilla numbers increasing or decreasing now?

Natural History

Donate Now

Skills Development
Writing
Describing

1.22   Writing Skills

1. About yourself

Write a paragraph giving information about yourself including your age, your address, and what you do.

Use the verbs *to be, to have,* and *to live* in the present tense, both in simple and continuous forms.

Practice using conjunctions and prepositions.

_____

_____

_____

_____

_____

2.   About your week

You receive e-mail from your friend asking you about your week. Reply to him or her, identifying the thing you did or saw.

Use the past tense, in both the simple and continuous form. Use the verbs *to go, to do,* and *to see.*

Practice using the conjunctions and prepositions.

_____

_____

_____

_____

_____

1.23   Review Exercises

Noun and verb agreement:

Complete the following:

1.   There _____(is, are) many sunny days in the month of July.

2.   The weather in June _____ (is, are) hot.

3.   The students _____ (is, are) studying physics.

4.   Physics_____ (is, are) a difficult subject.

5.   Each of the students _____ (has, have) a student card.

6.   Everyone _____ (has, have) a student card.

7.   The school furniture_____ (is, are) old.

8.   Neither of us_____ (is, are) going to the party.

9.   Either Jane or Mary _____ (has, have) it.

10. There _____ (is, are) a lot of rain today.

11. There _____ (is, are) a lot of people here.

12. Some of the work_____ (is, are) is hard.

13. The Japanese _____ (is, are) hardworking people.

14. French cars _____ (is, are) good.

15. Chinese _____ (is, are) a difficult language.

16. The number of students in the class_____ (is, are) small.

17. Twenty minutes _____ (is, are) a long time to wait.

18. Two hundred miles _____ (is, are) far away.

19. Many people_____ (like, likes) going on vacation.

20. A lot of the equipment _____ (is, are) faulty.

21. The information _____ (is, are) correct.

22. The news _____ (is, are) on at six.

23. Everybody _____ (is, are) here.

24. No one _____ (is, are) here.

25. None of the computers _____ (is, are) working.

26. A number of courses _____ (is, are) offered by the university.

27. Each man, woman, and child _____ (is, are) important.

28. Neither of them _____ (like, likes) to study.

Complete the following sentences by choosing the appropriate verb:

1. Some of my friends_____ (know, knows) the answer. For me, some of the homework_____ (is, are) difficult.

2. Usually a lot rain_____ (falls, fall) in the month of August. A lot of us _____ (get, gets) wet.

3. A number of teachers_____(speaks, speak) clearly. Some of them _____ (speak, speaks) quietly.

4. The number of students in the history class _____ (fall, falls) every year. Much of the work _____ (bore, bores) the students.

5. Much of the furniture_____ (need, needs) to be replaced. Some of the furniture _____ (is, are) good.

6. A lot of us _____ (travel, travels) every day by bus. Many of us _____ (arrive, arrives) at school on time.

7. Everybody _____ (loves, love) vacations. Many of us_____ (take, takes) vacations from work.

8. No one _____ (come, comes) here. Sometimes someone _____ (come, comes).

9. Everyone_____ (visit, visits) the mall on Sundays.

10. Everybody _____ (feel, feels) sad sometimes.

Complete the following sentences using the verbs in parentheses:

Use the present simple or continuous tense.

1. A lot of us_____ (to go) _____.

2. Everyone in my class _____ (to study) _____.

3. The Spanish language _____ (to be) _____.

4. Spanish people_____ (to like) _____.

5. Much of the news _____ (to contain) _____.

6. A lot of information_____ (to be) _____.

7. The number of people in the world (to increase)_____.

8. The group of scientists _____ (to travel) _____.

9. A large number of people _____ (to look at) _____.

10. Many of them_____ (to watch) _____.

Fill in the blanks with the appropriate verb and preposition.

1. We _____there (negative *to be*) when he _____ (to arrive). We were _____work.

2. _____ it great! (negative *to be*). We are going _____ a boat.

3. _____ we lucky! (negative *to be*). We are going_____a cruise ship.

4. _____ Sundays we usually go to church. Last Sunday we _____ (negative *to go*) we_____ (*to stay*) _____ home.

5. My friend_____(negative to have) a dime. Fortunately he_____ (to get) a job. He is starting his job_____ June.

6. We _____ (negative to have) much time. We need to be there _____ 6:00 PM.

7. Finally they _____ (to decide) they _____ (negative go) to the farm. They_____ (to remain) _____the city _____a hotel.

8. I _____ born _____ the tenth _____March _____the year 1997.

9. Mary and Tom _____ (negative to have) a house. They live_____ an apartment_____Avenida Rosa _____ number eight.

10. We _____ (negative to be) happy with the house. We _____ (to want) a bigger house with more rooms.

11. I _____ (to attend) university _____ 1999 _____ 2004.

12. I _____ (to live) _____ the city. _____ the moment I am working _____ nights.

13. _____ 1924, they _____ (to come) to America and settled _____ the East Coast.

14. We _____ (negative to like) the city. We liked living _____ the suburbs.

15. _____ weekends we go to the beach.

Convert the following to the passive:

1. People all over the world are wearing T-shirts.

   _____

2. Many children are drinking sodas.

   _____

3. Many factories in France are making wine.

   _____

4. The clown was amusing the children.

   _____

5. The long lecture was tiring them.

   _____

6. Many people are buying houses.

   _____

7. Many people are visiting the museum.

   _____

8. Everyone is watching the game.

   _____

9. Everyone is enjoying the holiday.

    _____

10. The falling rain is wetting the trees.

    _____

CHAPTER 2

📖 **Describing**

📖 **Comparing**

📖 **Locating**

> **Skills Development**
> **Grammar & Exercises**
> **Pronouns & Adjectives**

2.0 Replacing Nouns with Pronouns

We begin with a look at pronouns. Remember pronouns replace nouns.

Table 9: Types of pronouns

SUBJECT		OBJECT		RELATIVE	POSSESSIVE	RECIPROCAL	REFLEXIVE
I	We	Me	Us	Which	Ours	Myself	Each other
You	You	You	You	Whose	Yours	Yourself	
He/She	They	Him/Her	Them	Who	His/Hers	Herself	
It		It		Whom	Theirs	Himself	
					Its	Itself	
					Mine	Ourselves	
						Yourselves	
						Themselves	

2.1 The Subject, Object, and Possessive Pronouns

1. The subject pronoun replaces the subject noun.

Example:

a. Manuel is a good student.　　　He is a good student.

b.   The book was on the table   It was on the table.

c.   Mary and Jane are going to school.   They are going to school.

2.   The object pronoun replaces the object of the noun.

Example:

a.   I am going to see Mary and Jane.   I am going to see them.

b.   She is going to see Tom.   She is going to see him.

3.   Possessive pronouns suggest ownership.

Mine

Yours, his, hers, theirs

Ours

Example

a.   Whose pen is it?   It is mine.

b.   Is this yours?   No. It is hers.

c.   Whose house is it?   It is his.

d.   Who is he?   He is a friend of mine.

e.   Who are they?   They are some friends of ours.

> Unlike possessive nouns, possessive pronouns do not require apostrophes *(its, hers, theirs, ours, yours)*.

Example:

a.   The tree is dropping its leaves.

b.   Hers is the house at the end of the street.

c.   Yours is the one we chose.

2.2   Pronoun Agreement

2.2.1   Agreement with the Singular and Plural

The rules follow the same pattern as nouns.

Example:

1.   He lives in Argentina.

2.   They are very rich.

3.   It is on the table.

4.   She does her homework every night.

5.   They do everything in the house.

6.   He has a car.

7.   They have many cars.

Exercise 2.2a Practice the pronouns by filling in the blanks.

a.   Jane is going to school.

_____ is going to school.

b.   Andy is cleaning the car.

_____ is cleaning the car.

c.   The book is on the table.

_____ is on the table.

d.   The flight is going to Sweden.

_____ is going to Sweden.

e.   I am going to see my aunt.

I am going to see _____.

f.   I am going to visit my friends.

I am going to visit _____.

g.   The red car is my car.

     _____ is _____.

h.   The pen does not belong to you.

     _____ is not _____.

i.   The gray house belongs to us.

     _____ is _____.

j.   The house belongs to the couple.

     _____ belongs to _____.

     _____ is _____.

2.2.2   Agreement with the Collective Noun

A pronoun with a collective noun is singular. Collective nouns are singular.

Example:

1.   My family is small. It is made up of four persons.

2.   The staff works hard. It is a good staff.

Now consider where a collective noun refers to several persons. The pronoun is plural.

1.   My family is loving and caring. They are wonderful.

2.   The staff is having lunch at the Chinese restaurant. They work hard.

3.   The class is small. They are going to the game.

Exercise 2.2b Find a suitable pronoun for the following collective nouns.

a.   The football team was large. _____ was made up of nine people.

b.   The group went to Mexico. _____was made up of nine women.

c.   The group was tired. _____ needed to rest.

d.   The team was working hard. _____practiced every day.

e.   My family is planning a vacation. _____ are going to Miami.

f.   The group of lions is resting under the tree. _____look tired.

g.   My family is moving to a new house. _____ are looking forward to it.

h.   The staff has the day off. _____ are going to the games.

i.   The English class is small. _____ is up made of ten persons.

j.   The Spanish team is going home. _____lost the match.

2.2.3   Agreement with the Indefinite Pronoun

Indefinite pronouns are non-specific and are singular.

Everyone	Someone	Anyone	No one
Everybody	Somebody	Anybody	Nobody
Everything	Something	Anything	Nothing

Example

1.   Everyone is working.

2.   Everyone is going to school.

3.   Everything is fine.

4.   Everyone is free to choose.

5.   Every one of them is bright.

6.   Someone is in the bar.

7.   There is something on your shirt.

8.   He does not want anything.

9.   Is anyone at home?

Some indefinite pronouns are plural.

Both	Few	Many	Several

1. There are few left.

2. Both are coming to dinner.

3. Many are successful.

4. Several are leaving the party.

Exercise 2.2c Make the indefinite pronouns agree with the verbs in the present tense.

a. Everyone _____ a house. (to have)

b. Everything in here _____ dirty. (to be)

c. Someone _____his book. (to have)

d. Somebody _____ his keys. (to have)

e. No one _____ here! (to be)

f. Everybody _____ to the fair. (to go)

g. _____anyone seen my bag? (to have)

h. Everything _____ fine with me. (to be)

i. Many _____ the party. (to leave)

j. Both _____ to the party. (to come)

2.2.4 Agreement with the Indefinite Pronoun and the Antecedent

Examples:

1. Everyone has <u>his</u> own car.

2. Someone in the bar left <u>his</u> lights on.

3. Everyone is free to make <u>his</u> choice.

4. Everyone passed <u>his</u> exam.

5. Several of the houses have <u>their</u> own security alarms.

6. Many have <u>their</u> own homes.

7.   Anyone can park <u>his</u> car there.

8.   No one is allowed to park <u>his</u> car there.

Exercise 2.2d Fill in the blanks with the appropriate pronoun.

a.   Someone is driving _____ car too fast.

b.   Everyone has _____ work to do.

c.   Everyone went _____ way.

d.   Many need _____ salaries.

e.   Both of them are using _____ vehicles today.

f.   Anyone can have _____ house painted.

g.   Several of them got _____ visas.

h.   Many of them are losing _____ jobs.

i.   A few will keep _____ jobs.

j.   Both are returning to _____ countries.

2.3   The Reciprocal Pronouns

The pronoun must complement the plural subject.

The people in my class like each other.

Let's meet each other after dinner.

They love each other.

2.4   The Reflexive Pronouns

In such a case, the subject and the complement are the same.

Example:

1. I taught myself math.

2. I can do it myself.

3. She painted it herself.

4. She sits by herself.

5. We must thank ourselves for a job well done.

6. I see myself in the mirror each day.

"You drew that picture yourself?"
"Yes, I did it myself."

Exercise 2.4a Fill in the blanks with the suitable reflexive pronoun.

a.   I painted the wall _____.

b.   I always study by _____.

c.   He introduced _____ to me.

d.   They built the entire house by _____.

e.   She is always alone. She likes being by _____.

f.   Stop feeling sorry for _____!

g.   We need to examine _____ every day.

h.   Mrs. Brown is always talking to _____.

i.   We like being by _____.

j.   She is always looking at _____ in the mirror.

2.5   **Prepositions and Object Pronouns**

Prepositions are usually followed by the object pronoun.

Among (us)	Between (you and me)	For	From	to	with	of

➥Example

1.   Between you and me, I am tired of this food. I am tired <u>of it</u>.

2.   I am giving the book to Tom. I am giving the book <u>to him</u>.

3.   Mary likes studying with Jack. Mary likes studying <u>with him</u>.

4.   Mario lives with his mother. Mario lives <u>with her</u>.

5.   This present is from her <u>to him</u>.

6.   This is <u>for her</u>.

7.   There are many persons <u>among us</u>.

Exercise 2.5a Fill in the blanks with the appropriate pronoun.

a.   Mary and I are studying English. I am studying with _____.

b.   Between you and _____, this food is horrible.

c.   This book belongs to Alicia. I am taking it to _____.

d.   Are you taking the package to John? Yes, I am taking it to _____ now.

e.   Among _____ are many good students.

f.   Andy is buying a wedding ring for_____.

g.   I am tired of the food. I am tired of _____.

h.   The memo came from the boss. It came from _____.

i.   Jane got e-mail from Andy. She got e-mail from _____.

j.   Andy sent an e-mail to Jane. He sent an e-mail to _____.

2.6   The Interrogative Pronouns

These are question words (see chapter 1). Let's look at the examples again.

1.   Who are you?

2.   What did he say?

3.   Whose is it?

4.   Which of these are yours?

2.7   The Demonstrative Pronouns

This, that, these, and *those* are demonstrative pronouns used to replace ideas or things that are understood. Look at the examples below.

1.   Honesty is important to one's character. <u>This</u> makes us better people.

2.   Meditation is important to one's health. <u>That</u> is one way to relax.

3.   People can travel by plane, bus, or train. <u>These</u> are all means of transport.

4.   <u>This</u> is larger than <u>that.</u>

2.8   The Relative Pronouns

Who, whom, whose, which, and *that* are relative pronouns used to join sentences (i.e. they are conjunctive in function). They form adjective clauses.

Who, whom refers to a person, and *which* refers to a thing.

That is often used to replace *which. That* can be used for both persons and things.

Whose denotes possession by a person.

NB/Whom is formal and rarely used.

Examples:

a.   *Who, which,* and *that* (used as the subject of the verb)

Who	
I met the boy. He won the medal.	I met the boy <u>who won the medal</u>.
My father is a doctor. He works long hours.	My father <u>is a doctor who works long hours</u>.
Which, That	
The pen is mine. It fell on the ground.	The pen, <u>which fell on the ground,</u> is mine.
	The pen <u>that fell on the ground</u> is mine.

b.   *Whom, which,* and *that* (used as the object of the verb)

Whom, That	
We saw the man yesterday. It was Mr. Thomas.	The man <u>whom we saw</u> yesterday was Mr. Thomas.
	The man <u>that we saw</u> yesterday was Mr. Thomas.
Which, That	
I read the book. It was good.	The book, <u>which I read,</u> was good.
	The book <u>that I read</u> was good.

In these cases *that, which,* and *whom* can be omitted.

–   The book I read was good.

–   The boy I met won the race.

–   The man we saw yesterday was Mr. Thomas.

The subject of the verb cannot be omitted.

c.   *Whose*

Whose	
I met the woman. Her husband is the manager of the bank.	I met the woman whose husband is the manager of the bank

Now join the sentences below using the pronouns in parentheses. Use any combination or pattern you wish.

a.   My aunt is a doctor. She lives in America. (who)

b.   I apologized to the man. I stepped on his foot. (whose)

c.   The book is mine. It is new. (that)

d.   The man is her husband. I saw him. (that)

e.   I met the lady. She is the president of the company. (whom, who)

f.   She is wearing a dress. It is brand new. (which)

g.   We met the man. He is a well-known doctor. (who)

h.   The book fell on the ground. It is mine. (that)

i.   I met her at a party. The lady who is standing near the table. (whom)

j.   I like the desk. It is made of wood. (which)

Exercise 2.8a Fill in the blanks using *who, whom, which, that,* and *whose.*

1.   The lady at the corner of the room is the lady _____ I met last Saturday.

I was very happy to have met her.

She is the lady _____ gave me money to take a taxi when my car broke down.

The taxi _____ I took dropped me in front of my house.

2. My aunt _____ husband is a wealthy businessman took me shopping yesterday.

    She bought many things for me. The thing _____ I liked most was the red jacket.

Exercise 2.8b Join the sentences using relative pronouns.

a. The lady is having lunch. I borrowed her car.

b. I saw the boy. He won the race.

c. I have an aunt. Her son is a wealthy businessman.

d. I have a brother. He lives in the United States.

e. I read the book. It was good.

f. The man is very rich. I met him at the party.

g. He is the man. He helped me with my car.

h. This is the computer. It crashes all the time.

i. She is the lady. I met her on Sunday.

j. The sound was strange. We heard it.

Exercise 2.8c Join the sentences below into one sentence.

Use the first sentence as the adjective clause.

For example: My aunt is a doctor. She spends long hours at the hospital.

My aunt who is a doctor spends long hours at the hospital.

Use the second sentence as the adjective clause.

My aunt is a doctor who spends long hours at the hospital.

1. My father is an accountant. He spends long hours at the office.

2. My sister is a nurse. She is caring and helpful.

3. My brother is a politician. He is very ambitious.

Skills Development
Oral Skills
Q & A

2.9   Student Dialogue

Let's practice the pronouns.

Ask your classmate a simple question. Write the answers down.

Student a	Which is the best baseball team in the world?
Student b	
Student a	Do you know the team that won the last World Cup?
Student b	
Student a	Do you go out by yourself or with someone else?
Student b	
Student a	Whose books are those?
Student b	
Student a	Do you and your neighbors like each other?
Student b	
Student a	Hey! I found a pen. Is it yours or hers?
Student b	
Student a	Between you and me, do you like health foods?
Student b	
Student a	Computer science is an important subject. Do you agree with that?
Student b	
Student a	Does everyone in your family go on vacation?
Student b	

Student a	Who is the person who won the last presidential elections in your country?
Student b	
Student a	Which country in the world is famous for French food?
Student b	
Student a	Name a movie that you saw and liked.
Student b	
Student a	Name a book that you read and liked.
Student b	

Find the answers to these simple questions.

a.   Do you like everyone at school?

b.   Is there someone special that you like?

c.   Is anyone living with you at home?

d.   Did you see something in the shop to buy?

e.   Is there anything special you like to eat?

f.   Do you study by yourself or with someone?

g.   Whose house do you live in?

h.   Do you have a best friend? Who is he/she?

i.   Many students have a favorite subject. Which is yours?

j.   The English language is an important language. Do you agree with that?

2.10   Reviewing Adjectives

Adjectives are used to describe nouns and pronouns.

There are many types of adjectives. Let's look at them.

(Source: Nesfield's English Grammar, Caribbean Educational Publ, 1998)

Adjectives of description	
a red dress	a person—nice, happy, friendly, helpful
an old man	an early train
a fast train	a good car
Proper adjectives	
He is Chinese. (Nationality)	She is British.
Adjectives of possession	
My book	Her pen
Adjectives of quantity	
any, little, much	There is little rain today.
He has much money	He did not eat any food.
Numeral adjectives. Cardinal and Ordinal numbers	
I want five apples and three oranges.	My birthday is on the tenth of May.
The indefinite numeral	
Some, all, many, several, few.	Some people have money.
The interrogative adjective	
Which desk is yours?	What book is that?
The demonstrative adjective	
These, those, this, that.	These apples are good. Those oranges are sour.
This book is good.	That man is quite odd.
This house is old and that (house) is new.	
The adjectives of comparison. (See further details).	

"Do you want these apples or those bananas?"

Identify the adjective and the type of adjective in each sentence below. Make sure you can identify the nouns first. Remember adjectives qualify nouns.

a.   There is little food left in the cupboard.

b.   I like this red dress but not that yellow jacket.

c.   I don't have any money.

d.   I love French fashions.

e.   Marcelle is French. He is from France.

f.   This house is our house.

g.   I want five of these apples and three of those melons.

h.   There is much snow on the mountains.

i.   He is a young man.

j.   It is my pen.

Let's look at the following demonstrative adjectives again:

That	this	these	those

these	those
Who are these people?	Who were those people?

this	that
This pen is not writing.	Who was that man?

Let's practice using the demonstrative adjectives. Fill in the blanks.

that	this	these	those

a. Who is _____ man over there?

b. Who are _____ people here? Who are _____ people over there?

c. Can I have five of _____ oranges and five of _____ apples?

d. I don't like _____ place. Can we leave?

e. _____ place was noisy. _____ place is better.

f. _____ books are mine.

g. _____ book belongs to Amy.

h. Do you see the gray house over there? _____ house is my house.

i. Is _____ pen yours?

j. This bag is my bag. Is _____ your bag over there?

Let's look at some nouns.

book	money	rain	shoe	car	people
house	shop	building	food	dog	fashions
perfume	man	bed	garden	sea	carpet

Now find a suitable adjective to describe the nouns above.

Make sentences in the past tense using the following types of adjectives.

a) an adjective of description

b) an adjective of quantity

c) an adjective of possession

d) an adjective of demonstration

2.11   Using the Adjectives of Comparison
The Positive, Comparative, and Superlative

1.   Regular adjectives

We can form the comparative and superlative by adding -er to the positive and -est to the superlative. The comparative compares two things or two persons. The superlative refers to more that two.

Table 10: Comparative of regular adjectives

Positive	Comparative	Superlative
nice	nicer	nicest
pretty	prettier	prettiest
old	older	oldest
young	younger	youngest
tall	taller	tallest
short	shorter	shortest
big	bigger	biggest
small	smaller	smallest
smart	smartest	smartest
bright	brighter	brightest
large	larger	largest
fat	fatter	fattest
rich	richer	richest
lazy	lazier	laziest
busy	busier	busiest
easy	easier	easiest
cheap	cheaper	cheapest
wet	wetter	wettest
dry	drier	driest
hungry	hungrier	hungriest
angry	angrier	angriest
near	nearer	nearest

Let's look at some examples.

1.   Antonio is the youngest person in the family.

2. Antonio is my younger brother.

3. Antonio is younger than I.

4. Francesca is my older sister.

5. The shops in the town are cheaper shops than those in the mall.

6. He is the tallest boy in the class.

7. The city streets are the busiest streets in the country.

2. The irregular adjectives

In these cases, the comparative and superlative are not formed by adding -*er* or -*est* as above.

They are irregular.

Table 11: The positive, comparative, and superlative of the irregular adjectives

Positive	Comparative	Superlative
good	better	best
bad	worse	worst
little	less	least
much	more	most
many	more	most
few	fewer	fewest

Let's look at some examples.

1. We need better books in the class.

2. He is a good man.

3. It is a better school.

4. He is a bad man.

5. This is the worst food.

6. I have little money.

7. My mother has less money than I.

3.   Using *more* and *most*

Table 12: *More* and *most* as the comparative and superlative

Positive	Comparative	Superlative
beautiful	more beautiful	most beautiful
important	more important	most important
able	more able	most able
difficult	more difficult	most difficult
expensive	more expensive	most expensive
famous	more famous	most famous

Example

Let's look at some examples.

1.   School is the most important thing in a young person's life.

2.   She is the most beautiful girl in the class.

3.   He has a more expensive car than I do.

4.   School work is a more difficult thing than playing sports.

4.   Using the verb *to get* with the adjective

She is getting fat.	She is getting fatter.
He is getting tall.	He is getting taller.
He is getting hungry.	He is getting hungrier.
The soil is getting dry.	The soil is getting drier.

Note: Where the positive ends in -*y* and is preceded by a consonant, -*er* becomes -*ier* and *est* becomes –*iest* (for example, *dry, drier, driest*).

2.12   Using Adverbs

Simple adverbs of description

1.   She speaks quietly.

2.   He speaks loudly.

3.   She smiles brightly.

4.   He walks slowly.

5.   She dresses neatly.

6.   He is neatly dressed. (Example of an adverb used as an adjective)

Exercise 2.12a Write descriptive sentences using the verb *to get* with the adjective.

old   big   tall   hungry   thirsty   angry

Exercise 2.12b Complete the following sentences using the words below:

better   younger   least   tallest   best   more   richest   brightest   fastest

a.   We need _____ books in this school.

b.   He is _____ than his brother.

c.   He is the _____ boy in the class.

d.   They sell the _____ clothes.

e.   She has the _____ weight of all the girls.

f.   The exam was _____ difficult than we thought.

g.   In his family he is the _____ person.

h.   She is the _____ girl in the class.

i.   Her dress is _____ expensive than mine.

j.   His car is the _____ car.

Exercise 2.12c Fill in the blanks with the suitable pronoun to match the comparative adjective.

I   her   him   hers   theirs   ours   yours   mine

a.   He is older than his brother. He is older than_____.

b.   She is taller than her mother. Her mother is shorter than _____.

c.   My work is better than your work. My work is better than _____.

d.   I was late. He got to work earlier than _____.

e.   I am ten years old and my sister is five. She is younger than _____.

f.   Their garden is big. Our garden is smaller than _____.

g.   Our garden is big. Their garden is smaller than _____.

h.   Her house is large. My house is smaller than _____.

i.   This is her desk. This is my desk. Her desk is messier than _____.

j.   My car is cheap. His car is more expressive than _____.

Exercise 2.12d Fill in the blanks using the following.

a   an   and   but   can   has   have   she   is   who   on   there   at   to

I have_____ big family. I have a younger brother. He_____five years old and his name is Pepe. I also have _____ older sister. Her name is Maria._____ is twelve and I am eleven. My grandfather _____ lives with us helps us with many things.

He likes to work in the garden. My father is a salesman_____my mother is a teacher.

Maria wants to be an artist because she_____draw_____ my father thinks she should do something better.

_____ weekends we all go_____the beach where_____are many things to do. We always _____fun at the beach.

Skills Development
Oral Skills
Q&A

2.13   Student Dialogue

Let's practice the adjectives.

Ask your classmate a simple question. Write down the answers.

Student a	Which desk is your desk?
Student b	
Student a	Is that book your English book?
Student b	
Student a	Do you like Italian food?
Student b	
Student a	Do you have an older brother?
Student b	
Student a	Can you name a famous person?
Student b	
Student a	Do you like romantic movies or action movies?
Student b	
Student a	Which sport is more exciting? Bungee jumping or car racing?
Student b	
Student a	Which form of exercise is better? Swimming or running?
Student b	

Student a	Which do you like the most? Cable TV, music, or the Internet?
Student b	
Student a	Which book is the best book that you have read?
Student b	

Find the answers to these simple questions.

1. Are there many students in your class?

2. Do you always have homework?

3. Do you like reading the daily newspaper?

4. Do you like pop music?

5. Do you have a lot of friends or a few friends?

6. Do you like fast foods?

7. Do you like Latin dance?

8. What is your favorite TV channel?

9. What do you like about that channel?

10. Which is more important—education or sports?

2.14   Describing the Family

2.14.1   Using Adjectives and Adjective Clauses

Photo by Marty Casado

Vocabulary

General		
Employed	Self-employed	Unemployed
Married	Divorced	Single
Elder	Age	Twins
Baby	Toddler	Adult
Teen	Teenage	Teenager
Children	Adopted	Separated
Old	Young	Youth
Widow/er	Large	Small

People

Father	Mother	Grandfather	Grandmother
Brother	Sister	Half brother	Half sister
Husband	Wife	Brother-in-law	Sister-in-law
Father-in-law	Mother-in-law	Son-in-law	Daughter-in-law
Step father	Step mother	Grandson	Granddaughter
Nephew	Niece	Uncle	Aunt
Godfather	Godmother	Cousin	Family friend

Personality

Quiet	Angry	Serious	Kind
Loving	Jovial	Nervous	Caring
Studious	Worried	Disgusting	Ambitious
Happy	Beautiful	Hardworking	Smart
Gentle	Talented	Simple	Friendly
Unfriendly	Lazy	Honest	Helpful

Physical description

Tall	Short	Colour of hair
Fat	Thin	Colour of eyes
Skin tone	Pretty	Attractive
Neat	Well-dressed	Fit

Let's look at some examples.

1. He has brown hair.

2. She is a pretty lady.

3. He is a tall man.

4. He is a kind man.

5. He speaks quietly.

6. She is a happy girl.

Look at the photograph. List four things about him.

1._____   2._____

3._____   4._____

Exercise 2.14a Describe the members of your family.

In your descriptions, include physical characteristics and personality traits.

Use the adjectives of comparison (e.g. younger, older, best, etc.).

My mother   _____

_____

_____

My father _____

_____

_____

My sister _____

_____

_____

My stepfather _____

_____

_____

2.14.2   <u>What Do They Do?</u>

Nurse	_____	Lawyer	_____
Doctor	_____	Engineer	_____
Businessman	_____	Teacher	_____
Flight Attendant	_____	Pilot	_____
Manager	_____	Secretary	_____
Policeman	_____	Accountant	_____

Adding relative clauses

Examples:

1.   My brother who is a lawyer lives in Texas. (present tense)

2.   My sister who is younger than I likes to study.

3.   He is a doctor who works all day.

3.   He is an engineer who travels all over the world.

4.   She was a nurse who worked hard. (past tense)

5.   They were teachers whose students did well.

Exercise 2.14b Make simple sentences describing what family members do.

Use the relative pronouns *who, whose.*

a.   My father   _____

b.   My mother _____

c.   My aunt   _____

d.   My uncle   _____

e.   My sister   _____

f.   My stepfather _____

2.14.3   Family Activities

<u>A Wedding</u>

Photo courtesy Tradewind Tours Jamaica

FAMILY CELEBRATIONS

birthdays	Christmas
funerals	baptism
New Year's Day	Easter
weddings	anniversary

ACTIVITIES

studying	reading	swimming
cooking	painting	sports
listening to music	poetry	dancing
gardening	shopping	camping
looking at television	going to church	going to a concert
dining at a restaurant	visiting friends and family	painting the house

FREQUENCY

often	never
sometimes	always
We never go dancing.	
We always go dancing. shopping.	
Sometimes we go shopping.	

What activities do you share?

Let's look at some examples.

1. We enjoy spending time with each other.

2. We often have dinner together.

3. On Sundays someone usually visits us. We like having friends.

4. We sometimes go to the beach on weekends.

5. We always go shopping together.

6. Everyone enjoys listening to music.

7. Everybody watches television.

Exercise 2.14c List some of the activities that you and your family do together.

1. _____   2. _____

3. _____   4. _____

5. _____   6. _____

Exercise 2.14d Write sentences about yourself and your family. In making sentences, remember to combine short sentences. Practice using adjectives of comparison and relative clauses. Look at the examples below:

1. I like eating good food, but I hate cooking. My mother, who is at home all the time, cooks my dinner. She is a great cook. Sundays are best. She either bakes a chicken or cooks lamp chops.

2. I like spending time with my family. My father, who is a lawyer, works very hard but on weekends he stays at home. Sometimes we go to the beach. Often we eat dinner together and watch a comedy on cable TV.

3. I like going to the gym. Neither my younger sister Jane nor my older brother Larry goes with me. They like watching movies on the cable channels and eating junk food. I don't like junk food. I like vegetables and fruits.

1. _____

_____

_____

2. _____

_____

_____

3. _____

_____

_____

2.14.4   Likes and Dislikes

Likes	
I like reading books.	I like watching cable TV.
I like studying.	I like the Internet.
I like sports.	I like being with my family.

Using the adverbs *more* and *most*:

More	
I like coffee and tea.	I like coffee more.

Most
I like history and math, but I like English most.

Make a list of the things you like. Try using the comparative *more* and *most*.

_____   _____

_____   _____

_____   _____

_____   _____

Dislikes	
I don't like housework.	I don't like vegetables.
I don't like schoolwork.	I don't like the weather.
I don't like being by myself.	I don't like sports.

Make a list of things you don't like.

_____

_____

_____

At the movies…Do you like movies?

SHOWTIMES

| MOVIE SHOWTIMES | EVENT LISTINGS | CLASSIFIED ADS | SEARCH & ARCHIVES |

Adventure and romance

Beyond Borders : the present

Starring Angelina Jolie and Clive Owen.

Angelina Jolie is a beautiful young woman who plays the part of Sarah Jordan. She meets the star of the show, Nick Callahan, at a party and decides to go to Ethiopia with him to look after refugees and starving people. She takes all her money and leaves behind her husband. Eventually Sarah and Nick fall in love. The story is about adventure and romance.

What type of story is this? _____

The Ice Age : the past

This computer-animated feature is set during the ice age twenty thousand years ago when glaciers covered the Earth's surface. A wooly mammoth, a saber-toothed tiger, and a giant sloth happen upon a human infant. The prehistoric animals must work to overcome obstacles and take the child back to its parents.

What are the sub-zero heroes trying to do? _____

Matrix Revolutions : the future

Starring: Keanu Reeves, Carrie-Anne Moss, Laurence Fishburne, and Hugo Weaving

Cyberheroes Neo, Morpheus, and Trinity must defend the underground city of Zion as they face off against the artificial-intelligence machines in an ultimate showdown to prevent the extinction of the human race in the third and final chapter of *The Matrix* trilogy.

What are the cyberheroes trying to do? _____

Make a list of your favorite movies

1. _____   2. _____

3. _____   4. _____

5. _____   6. _____

7. _____   8. _____

9. _____   10. _____

Which do you like the most? _____

| Skills Development |
| Oral Skills |
| Conversation |

2.15   Conversation 4. Talking about the Family

Practice the conversations with a friend or classmate.

Situation 1

About your family.

Your friend invites you to spend a week with his family in Australia. Let's find out about them.

– Hi. Tell me about your family.

– I have a small family. My family is loving and caring. They are wonderful!

– Do you have many brothers and sisters?

– I have one brother, who is younger than I.

– Does your family like doing things together?

– Oh, yes! We go to dinner together; we go to the beach. We do many things together.

– I can't wait to meet them!

– And they are looking forward to meeting you!

Situation 2

Spending the weekend.

You meet your friend at the office. Find out about her weekend.

– Hello. What did you do for the weekend?

– My family and I went camping. We had a great time. What did you do?

– We spent the weekend at the beach.

– Whose house did you stay in?

– My uncle's house. He has a house on the beach in Margarita.

– Did you have a good time?

– A great time.

What do they do?

Someone wants to know about your family's profession. Tell him or her.

– Tell me about your family. What does your father do?

– My father is an accountant who likes to work all the time.

– How many brothers do you have?

– I have two brothers. They are lawyers.

– And your sister?

– I have a sister who is younger than I. She likes studying English.

– Who is your favorite aunt?

– My favorite aunt is Anita. She is a doctor who works very hard.

I met your cousin Lisa!

You met your friend's cousin at the shop. Tell her about the encounter.

– Hi. I met your cousin Lisa yesterday.

– You did? Lisa is a wonderful person. She is kind, honest, and fun to be with.

– What does she like doing?

– She likes many things. She likes going to the beach, playing tennis, meeting people and of course she likes her school.

– What is her favorite subject?

– She likes all her subjects, but she likes English the most.

– I think she is a wonderful person.

– Yes. She is.

> **Skills Development**
> **Writing**
> **Describing**

2.16   Writing Skills

1.   A wedding

Write a brief description of a wedding you attended.

> Note: Use adjectives, pronouns, and relative clauses. Use the past tense.

_____

_____

_____

_____

_____

_____

2.   The family

Write a paragraph describing your family. Give their ages, where they work, and describe their hobbies and their personalities. Describe the things you do together.

> Note: Use adjectives, pronouns, and relative clauses. Use the present tense.

_____

_____

_____

_____

_____

3. Your likes and dislikes

Write a paragraph about the things you like and don't like.

Use the adverbs *more* and *most* as comparisons.

_____

_____

_____

_____

_____

4. A movie

Write a brief and simple description about a movie you saw and liked.

Use the preposition *about* and the relative or adjective clauses *that* and *who*

_____

_____

_____

_____

_____

_____

Skills Development
Identifying

2.17   Identifying the Items in the House

THE KITCHEN		
table	spoons	microwave oven
chairs	pot and pans	pressure cooker
refrigerator	fryer	appliances
knives	steamer	forks

TABLE AND CHAIRS	THE DINING ROOM	LIVING ROOM

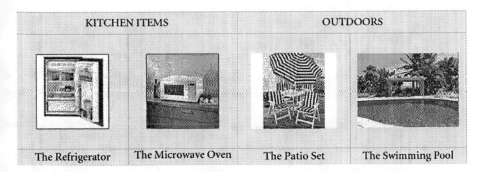

KITCHEN ITEMS		OUTDOORS	
The Refrigerator	The Microwave Oven	The Patio Set	The Swimming Pool

THE BEDROOM		
The bed	Lamp	Bedcover
Carpet	Desk and Chair	Curtains
Air conditioner	The cupboard	The side table

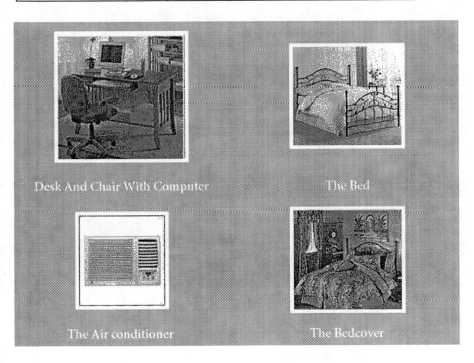

Desk And Chair With Computer

The Bed

The Air conditioner

The Bedcover

The Lamp   Armchair With Cupboard.

THE LIVING ROOM

furniture	sofa	television
armchair	carpet	stereo
video	coffee table	light switch

CLEANING THE HOUSE

vacuum	iron
broom	washing machine
laundry	dryer

THE OUTDOOR

patio	garden
swimming pool	fish pond

GARDEN TOOLS

lawn mower	rake
hose	hoe

What do you have in your house?

Write them down.

1. _____

2. _____

3. _____

4. _____

5. _____

6. _____

7. _____

8. _____

9. _____

10. _____

Skills Development
Grammar & Exercises
Prepositions
Locating

2.18   Prepositions

Vocabulary

apartment	floor	garage
dining room	door	window
bedroom	bathroom	garbage bin
living room	library	walls
porch	staircase	swimming pool
patio	tiles	counter
corridor	dresser	garden
roof	kitchen	study

Prepositions are usually followed by nouns and pronouns

by	to	among	between
with	from	for	near
of	across	along	next to
about			

Let's practice some examples.

1.   I am looking <u>for</u> the garden tools.

2.   I am going <u>to</u> the garden.

3.   The bed is <u>next to</u> the lamp.

4.   The kitchen is <u>near</u> the porch.

5.   We moved the dining set <u>from</u> the kitchen <u>to</u> the dining room.

6.   I am scrubbing the floor <u>with</u> detergent.

7. The garage is <u>along</u> the side <u>of</u> the house.

8. The garbage bin is just <u>across</u> the street.

9. He moves things <u>about</u> the house.

10. This room is used <u>for</u> storage.

Exercise 2.18a Fill in the blanks with the suitable preposition.

| with | next to | to | by | near | along | between | among | for |

a. The stereo is _____ the television.

b. He is studying _____ his friend in the library.

c. She is going _____ the laundry.

d. I am looking _____ the iron everywhere.

e. She was standing _____ the kitchen door.

f. The house is _____ the river.

g. The bedrooms are _____ the corridor.

h. The toilet is _____ the two bedrooms.

i. The clothes are _____ the pile.

j. The baby's room is _____ the master bedroom.

Exercise 2.18b Fill in the blanks with suitable prepositions.

| from | for | to | by | of |

a. The clothes are wet _____ the rain.

b. I need a photocopier _____ copy my book.

c. I need a photocopier _____ copying books.

d. We can go to Merida _____ bus.

e. I am going _____ a walk with my dog.

f. I am going out _____ walk my dog.

g. What type _____ car is it?

h.   We attended school _____1995 _____1999.

i.   We are far _____the station.

j.   We got to the party _____ taxi.

> Note: Common errors occur in the use of *for* and *to*.

Error: am going for to walk my dog.

Correction: I am going to walk my dog.

                  I am going for a walk with my dog.

Exercise 2.18c Fill in the blanks with the prepositions and object pronouns.

a.   There were many good people _____ us. (preposition)

b.   Between you and _____ that restaurant was expensive. (pronoun)

c.   He was buying a car for _____. (pronoun)

d.   I went _____him to the party. (preposition)

e.   He was buying a ring _____ her. (preposition)

f.   Mary and Candy were tired of eating the same food. They were tired of _____. (pronoun)

g.   I went to _____ about my school grades. (pronoun)

h.   I went with _____ to see the show. (pronoun)

i.   He talked all night _____them. (preposition)

j.   It was a gift from _____. (pronoun)

Exercise 2.18d Fill in the blanks in the short text using pronouns and prepositions.

in	at	on	next to	each other	with	it	her	him	to

Marisela Lopez lives_____an apartment_____the third floor of_____building. In her apartment there are many things but her favorite thing is the telephone. Marisela speaks _____ her friend David for hours.

At nights after dinner, she goes_____ her room to talk with_____. Maybe Marisela and David love _____.

Marisela's parents are never _____ home. They work quite late. _____Sundays they spend time together as a family. It is a small family. Marisela has one sister. She is ten years old. She sleeps often _____the home of her aunt. Her house is _____Marisela's house.

Marisela is always alone and she can do as she pleases. Sometimes she does her homework.

But really she does not like doing _____.

At 10:30 PM Marisela goes to bed. She gets up at 7:30 AM to go to school. The school bus arrives at 8:15 AM to take her to school. Her school is _____ Victoria Boulevard _____# 6.

Skills Development
Oral Skills
Q&A

2.19   Student Dialogue

Practice using the prepositions.

Ask your classmate a simple question. Write the answer down.

Student a	Do you live in a house or in an apartment?
Student b	
Student a	How many people live with you?
Student b	
Student a	What is next to the kitchen in your house?
Student b	
Student a	Is the refrigerator near the stove?
Student b	
Student a	Can you describe your house?
Student b	
Student a	What do you do? Do you work for a company?
Student b	
Student a	What do you like about your job?
Student b	
Student a	Is your office near your house?
Student b	

Student a	How do you get to work?
Student b	
Student a	Can you describe your office?
Student b	

Find the answers to these simple questions.

a.   Do you like watching television or reading at nights?

b.   Do you like swimming in the sea or swimming in a pool?

c.   Is the television on all day?

d.   Is your TV next to your bed?

e.   Do you sit for long hours at the computer?

f.   Do you live near the mall?

g.   Do you like going for walks in the park?

h.   Which country are you from?

i.   At weekends do you go to the beach?

j.   Do you have parties at your home?

Skills Development
Grammar & Exercises
Nouns & Verbs

2.20   Describing the House

Vocabulary

clean	old	simple
tidy	fancy	many
small	comfortable	few
big	spacious	new

1.   Using adjectives

Let's look at the examples.

–   The house is a large house.

–   It is a large and tidy house.

–   It is a white house.

–   There are many things in the house.

–   It is small.

2.   Using adjectives of comparison

large	larger	largest
small	smaller	smallest
clean	cleaner	cleanest
new	newer	newest
good	better	best
old	older	oldest
simple	simpler	simplest
big	bigger	biggest

Let's look at some examples.

—   The kitchen is larger than the bedroom.

—   The dining table is newer than the kitchen table.

—   The bedroom is cleaner than the kitchen.

3.   Using the irregular adjectives of comparison

good	better	best
bad	worse	worst
little	less	least

—   My house is better than hers.

—   I have the best house.

4.   Using *more* and *most*

More	Most
more expensive	most expensive
more spacious	most spacious
more luxurious	most luxurious
more comfortable	most comfortable

1.   My garden is the most beautiful garden.

2.   My house is the most spacious one.

3.   Jane's house is more luxurious than mine.

4.   My garden is more beautiful than hers.

5.   The bedroom is the most comfortable room.

Exercise 2.20a Write simple descriptive sentences about your house. Practice using adjectives of comparison and prepositions to locate items.

1.   _____

2.   _____

3.   _____

4. _____

5. _____

6. _____

Exercise 2.20b Fill in the blanks using the adjectives of comparison.

Larger	Bigger	Cleaner	Newer	Small	More expensive	More comfortable

a.   Jane's house is big. It is _____ than mine.

b.   My bedroom is clean. It is _____ than the kitchen.

c.   The kitchen is large. It is _____ than the TV room.

d.   I sold my old house and bought a _____ one.

e.   My dining table is expensive. It is _____ than the kitchen table.

f.   My new apartment is comfortable. It is _____ than my old apartment.

g.   My dining table is small. It is _____ than Jane's.

h.   The master bedroom is _____ than my bedroom.

i.   My house is filled with expensive items. They are _____ than yours.

j.   Her house is filled with new items. They are _____ than mine.

Skills Development
Oral Skills
Conversation

2.21   Conversation 5. Describing the House

Practice the conversation below or create similar conversations with your classmate.

Situation 1.

Tell me about your house.

Your friend is describing a house he lived in. Let's hear what he has to say.

—   Did you live in a house or in an apartment?

—   I lived in a big house with a garden and pool.

—   Did your house have many rooms?

—   My house had five bedrooms, two bathrooms, a dining room, a kitchen, and a living room.

—   What did you have in your kitchen?

—   There were many things in my kitchen. I had a fridge, a gas stove, a toaster, and a microwave.

—   And your bedroom?

—   In my bedroom there was a large bed. Next to my bed was a lamp and a desk for my computer.

—   Was your house air-conditioned?

—   Yes, it was.

Situation 2.

Tell me about your apartment.

Your friend has just found himself a new apartment. Ask him about it.

- Tell me about your apartment.

- My apartment is on Rose Avenue at #4. It is on the third floor. It is a small apartment. It is not fancy, but it is clean and comfortable.

- Do you have many things in your apartment?

- No I don't. I don't even have a telephone.

- Do you have a television, a radio, and stereo?

- No. All I have is a big bed, a fridge, and a stove at the moment.

Situation 3.

Comparing the houses

Your girlfriend just bought a new house. How does it compare with yours?

- Hi. Is this your new house? Let me have a look.

- Yes. Come in. This is the kitchen with all modern appliances.

- Very nice. My kitchen is bigger than yours. But my appliances are older.

- Come and see the garden. It is my favorite place. Isn't it lovely?

- Yes, it is clean and tidy. Your garden is better than ours.

- And let me show you the living room. It is spacious and comfortable.

- Yes, your living room is bigger than ours. Oh! It is late. I must go now.

Skills Development
Oral Skills
Role Plays

2.22　Role Play: Dealing with the Situation

1. You are having a birthday party. Call your friend and invite him or her.

2. Your friend is having a party. Call and find out what she needs for the party.

3. You wish to buy your friend a birthday gift. Find out what she wants.

4. You are at a restaurant with your family. Someone wants a bowl of soup. Ask for it.

5. Ask your friend about her/his favorite TV program.

6. Do you have a family pet? Do you like pets? How do you care for your pet?

7. You are looking for a house to buy. You meet someone with a house for sale. Introduce yourself and find out about the house. Ask about size, color, how many rooms, and where the house is situated.

8. You just bought a new home. What are the things you are going to buy?

9. Describe your dream house.

10. You are looking for an apartment to rent. Someone has an apartment to rent. Call and ask about it.

HOUSEWORK

Keeping a House Clean and Tidy Is Hard Work. You Can Help.

Mop the floor	Put away dishes
Clean the bathrooms	Clean the oven
Wash the dishes	Clean the refrigerator
Do the laundry	Put out the garbage
Sweep and vacuum	See about the garden
Cook	Clean windows
Wash the car	Bathe the dog
Clean the bedrooms	Do the groceries
Paint	Baby-sit

Make a list of the things you do at home.

1. _____   2. _____

3. _____   4. _____

5. _____   6. _____

Some useful verbs

To Paint	To Clean	To Bathe	
To Cook	To Put	To shop	

Make simple sentences using the verbs above.

1. _____

2. _____

3. _____

4. _____

5. _____

6. _____

Skills Development
Reading
Comprehension

2.23   Reading Comprehension

Read the following passages and answer the questions below.

2.23.1.   Work Begins at Home

According to Christine Field, your child's development begins at home. Children should do work at home. Here is what she suggests: First, children two to three years old can put their clothes on; children four to five years old can put groceries away, put dishes in the dishwasher, water plants, and set the table. Children between the ages of six to twelve should see about the pets, cook simple foods, see about the garbage, clean the bathroom, and tend to the garden among other things. Children over the age of thirteen can cook, clean the refrigerator, clean the oven, vacuum, polish and clean the car, and shop for groceries. This is important for a stable family life. It is important to teach your children responsibility at an early age. It is also very important that both boys and girls do housework such as cooking and cleaning.[6]

Now match the following.

1.	Children between the ages of four and five	A	Set the table
2.	Children between six and twelve years	B	Put their clothes on
3.	Children over thirteen should	C	See about the pets
4.	Children two to three years old	D	Clean the refrigerator

2.23.2.   The Boy from Bogota

Marcelo Pino lives in the city of Bogota in the country of Colombia. He is sixteen years old and very handsome. He is tall and tan with brown eyes and blonde hair. He lives in the barrio of Bogota with his mother and younger sister. Marcelo does not have a father. His father left them many years ago when Marcelo was a little boy at the age of three. His sister is fourteen years old, and her name is Consuelo. Consuelo goes to school every day. She is very intelligent and works very hard. Marcelo does not go to school. He and his mother work very hard selling fish in the market in Bogota. The money they earn pays the rent for their simple house and buys food, some clothes, and some books for Consuelo to go to school. They do not have much money but they love each other very much. Their house is simple and has two rooms and a small kitchen. There is no television and sometimes there are no lights and water. The kitchen has a table with four chairs.

One day Marcelo was walking home by himself when he met a poor old lady. She told him that she was very hungry and that she had no money.

"I can give you a fish, my lady," he said.

She smiled at him.

"Thank you, my boy," she said. "I will give you this."

"What is this?" he asked.

"It is a lotto ticket. You take it. Maybe you will win the lotto!"

"Thank you very much," he said. He took the ticket and continued walking home.

The next day was Saturday. It was the day of the lotto drawing. Marcelo Pino jumped for joy as he looked at the ticket in his hand. He looked at it one hundred times until he was sure. He still couldn't believe it. He couldn't believe that he had won the lotto! He was very happy. He won one million dollars!

Immediately Marcelo ran from his house onto the street where he had met the lady. Alas! There was no lady. He asked everyone around the barrio about her but no one ever saw the lady. Marcelo was very sad. He looked for her for many months but she was nowhere. It was strange. Who was she? he wondered.

Today Marcelo lives in a big house with a lovely garden and he drives a sports car. He has a refrigerator, a television, a video, air-conditioning, a stereo, a swimming pool, a gym, and a Jacuzzi. He also has water and lights all the time and a computer. Marcelo no longer lives in the rundown barrio. He lives in the rich part of the city. But he still looks for the old lady every day. He still thinks about her.

Check the items that Marcelo has in his new house.

Items	Yes	No	Items	Yes	No
furniture			air-conditioning		
television			swimming pool		
telephone			gym		
electricity			Jacuzzi		
water			sports car		
refrigerator			garden		
computer			video		

a.   Can you describe Marcelo Pino?

b.   Can you describe his old house?

c.   What happened to him one day?

d.   What did he win?

e.   How did he feel?

f.   What did he do after?

g.   Why does he want to find her?

2.23.3.   There Is a Mouse in My House

Mrs. Jones is very proud of her house. She is proud of her house because it is always neat, tidy, and clean. One day while she was cleaning the carpets, she saw a little mouse run across the kitchen floor. Mrs. Jones always boasted that mice are never found in her house—only in dirty houses. She was very upset and ashamed when she saw the mouse in her own house. She quickly called the pest company and spoke to them.

"A terrible thing has happened," she said. "I saw a mouse in my kitchen. Can you please come quickly? Hurry! I must get rid of it at once!"

"Calm down, Mrs. Jones," the man replied. "All right, I am coming to your house now with a mouse trap."

"Please," she said. "I must ask you a favor."

"What is it, Mrs. Jones?"

"Don't tell anybody!" she cried.

"No. I won't, Mrs. Jones."

a.   How did Mrs. Jones feel about her house?

b.   Why did she feel that way?

c.   What happened one day?

d.   What was she doing at the time?

e.   What did she tell other people?

f.   How did she feel?

g.   What did she do?

h.   What special favor did she ask for?

Skills Development
Writing an
Advertisement

2.24   Creating an Advertisement

Imagine you are selling a house. Using the example below as a guideline, create an advertisement for the newspaper.

BUYING A HOUSE?
We have just what you want!
Look at this fantastic offer!
Pool, tennis court, garden and patio, garage
swimming pool! five bedrooms!
Excellent price.
Call 1-800-589-2435

Skills Development
Listen and
Comprehend

2.25   Scripts 3, 4. Floor Plans.

Someone is needed to read Scripts 3 and 4 (appendices 2 and 3).

1. Look at the floor plan below. Listen to the speaker. It is someone
    describing a floor plan for an office. Listen to the speaker and identify
    the parts labeled A–H. (See appendix 2)

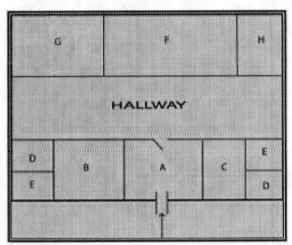

2. Listen to the speaker. He is advertising a house for sale. Listen to what
    he says. At the end of the talk, label the plans below as described. (See
    appendix 3.)

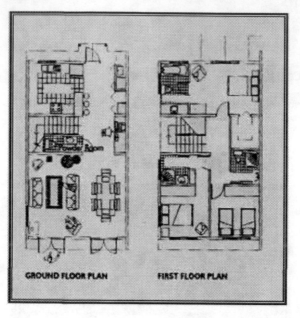

2.26   Review Exercises

Using a suitable pronoun, fill in the blanks below.

1. When I came home, I saw him sitting by_____. I asked him what was the matter. What he said was indeed sad. He said that the man_____borrowed all his money had disappeared forever.

2. I don't like being by_____. I am really a person_____ likes company. That is the reason why I called my friend Don. He is also at home by _____.

3. We built this house._____is why we are not very happy at the moment. The room _____is our favorite is the wrong color!

4. _____is absolute nonsense! You are not going on a trip to Africa by_____. It's too far. _____idea is this?

5. Lucy and Paul are two people_____love_____very much. Soon they will be married. The honeymoon that she chose was one in Hawaii. When they return they will live in a house _____he chose.

6. The house_____we like is big and spacious._____is situated on Apple Avenue. I want it to be our house, _____and mine.

7. I am buying a car for my wife. I am buying _____for _____because she needs to take the kids to school. In the evenings _____get home at four o'clock.

8. My garden is bigger than Mary's garden. _____is bigger than _____.

9. Their house is bigger than my house. My house is smaller than _____.

10. Our car is an old car. My neighbor's car is newer than _____.

Join the following sentences using the relative pronouns as conjunctions (*who, that, which, whose, whom*).

1. I like the car. It is very expensive.

2. The man came to see me. He is the new professor of English.

3. The man is living in England. I bought his house.

4.   I bought the blouse yesterday. It is too big.

5.   I spoke to the lady. She is the new decorator.

6.   The teacher teaches math. He is very popular with the students.

7.   The students were selected for the trip. They are leaving on Sunday.

8.   I like the big sofa. It is very comfortable.

9.   I met the man. He is the director of the new company.

10. I passed the exam. It was easy.

Review the comparatives and superlatives. Complete the sentences below:

1.   My brother is ten years old. I am five years old.

     I am _____.

     He is _____.

2.   I like tea, coffee, and orange juice.

     I like orange juice the _____.

     I like tea but I like coffee _____.

3.   Susanna, Clara, and Anna are all beautiful girls, but

     Susanna is the _____.

4.   I am five feet in height. My brother is six feet in height.

     He is _____.

     I am _____.

5.   Susanna, Clara, and Anna all dress well, but

     Clara is _____.

6.   All the kids are happy but Luisa is the _____.

7.   The soil gets dry in December. It is _____in March.

8.   None of us has money.

     I have the _____of all.

9. There are ten people in history class and fifty in the computer science class.

   There are _____ people in the history class.

10. I bought two cars. Both are expensive but the SUV is _____ than the sedan.

11. Tom and Larry both speak loudly. Larry speaks _____than Tom.

12. The food at the cafeteria is the _____ of all.

13. I like soccer and baseball. I like baseball _____.

14. The Italian restaurant is good, but the Chinese restaurant is _____.

Fill the blanks with the appropriate preposition.

1. We are leaving home _____ the city.

2. He is Canadian. He is _____Canada.

3. He is buying a house _____his mother.

4. They are going _____ the concert.

5. They spoke _____the movie.

6. He walks _____ the side of the dusty road.

7. She lives _____ the river.

8. She is saving her money _____a vacation.

9. You can pass _____ later.

10. He is standing _____ the doorway.

CHAPTER 3

📖 **Time and Weather**
📖 **Expressing Ability/Politeness**
   Adverb Clause of Time, Cause and Effect

> **Skills Development**
> **Grammar & Exercises**
> **Nouns, Adjectives,**
> **Verbs**

3.0   Time and Weather

Let's begin with a look at some key words and verbs.

Vocabulary

Key words

evening	morning	nighttime
sunrise	sunset	dawn
dusk	dinnertime	lunchtime
dusk	dinnertime	lunchtime
spring	autumn	summer
winter	fall	seasons
late	early	on-time
weather	rain	sunshine
snow	dark	light
thunder	storm	climate
wind	hot	cold
showers	temperature	clouds

Key verbs

to pour	to awaken	to rain
to get up	to be ready	to snow
to be late	to arrive	to freeze
to be early	to leave	to be hot
to hurry	to get to	be cold
to shine	to fall	to drizzle

3.1   Expressing Time

1.   Using the prepositions *on*, *at*, and *in*

The prepositional use can best be demonstrated by the use of examples.

a.   He gets up <u>at 4:00 AM</u>.

b.   He arrived <u>at 2:00 PM</u>.

c.   We go out for walks <u>on mornings</u>.

d.   <u>On evenings</u> we go to the park.

e.   <u>At nights</u> we sit and watch TV.

f.   <u>At the moment</u> we are having dinner.

g.   <u>On weekends</u> we go to the beach.

h.   We are going <u>in summer</u>.

> Note: Common error: *en este momento* is translated *at the moment*, not *in this moment*.

2.   Using *late*, *early*, *dark*, and *light*.

Time is often expressed as early, late, dark, and light.

Let's practice making some simple sentences.

Present tense (the verb to get)	
a. I am leaving. It is getting late.	He gets up early. He gets up at 5:00 AM.

Past tense (the verbs to awaken, to get)	
b. He awoke early. It was just getting light.	He got up late. The alarm did not go off.

Now practice making similar sentences.

Use the verbs *to get, to get up, to leave,* and *to arrive* in the present and past tense.

Use the verb *to go* in the future tense—*going to.*

Example: He is arriving early. He is not going to be late.

It is winter time. It gets dark early.

1. _____   2. _____

3. _____   4. _____

5. _____   6. _____

Now let's compare the adverb and the adjective.

Adverbs and adjectives can be used to describe and express time. Some words however have the same form but function differently. Adjectives describe nouns and pronouns. The adverb describes the verb.

Example:

Adverb	Adjective
a. He arrived late.	He arrived at a late hour.
b. He arrived early.	He took the early train.
c. He came early.	He had a late night.
d. He came late.	It is getting late.
e. The flight arrived on time.	It is getting dark.

Exercise 3.1a Now practice the use of *early* and *late* by making simple sentences.

Use the words as adjectives and adverbs.

1. _____

2. _____

3. _____

4. _____

5. _____

6. _____

3.2   Describing the Weather

The weather is often described in a number of ways by using nouns, adjectives, and verbs.

3.2.1. Using the Verbs

The verbs *to snow, to rain, to pour,* and *to shine* are often used to describe the weather.

Let's look at how they are used.

Present Tense	Past Tense
It rains every day.	It rained all day yesterday.
Present continuous	Past continuous
It is raining heavily.	It was raining all day yesterday.

Now practice making simple sentences using the verbs *to pour, to shine,* and *to snow.*

3.2.2. Using Adjectives and Nouns

Adjectives and nouns are commonly used to describe the weather.

Table 13: Adjectives and nouns compared

Adjective	Noun
snowy	snow
rainy	rain
showery	showers
sunny	sun
cloudy	cloud
windy	wind
foggy	fog

Let's look at some examples of the use of verbs, adjectives, and nouns.

a.   It is <u>snowing (verb)</u>. It is a <u>snowy (adjective)</u> day. There is a lot of <u>snow (noun)</u> today.

b.   It is a <u>windy</u> day. There is a lot of <u>wind</u> today.

c.   It is <u>raining.</u> It is a <u>rainy</u> day. There is a lot of <u>rain</u> today.

Look at the photos below.

It is raining.

It is snowing.

It is sunny.

The Weather Is Bad. Photo by Marty Casado

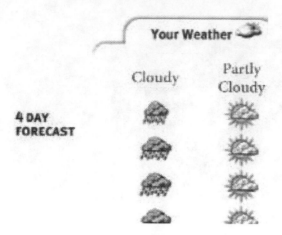

3.2.3 Using Comparatives and Superlatives

Table 14: The positive, comparative, and superlative of some common words.

Positive	Comparative	Superlative
hot	hotter	hottest
cool	cooler	coolest
warm	warmer	warmest
cold	colder	coldest
sunny	sunnier	sunniest

Examples:

Let's look at some examples.

1. It is hot.

2. It is hotter today than yesterday.

3. Yesterday was the coolest day of the year.

4. I feel cooler with the air-conditioning on.

5. It is getting warmer.

Exercise 3.2a Fill in the blanks with the suitable noun, verb, adjective.

a. The sun is _____. It is a _____ day. There is a lot of
    _____ today.

b.   It is _____. It is a rainy day. There is a lot of _____today.

c.   It is a _____ day. There is a lot of _____today.

d.   I can't see where I am going. It is _____today. There is a lot of_____.

e.   There is a storm out at sea. The sea is _____ today.

f.   I am sweating! It is _____.

g.   I am freezing! It is _____.

h.   The rain is _____ all day.

i.   It is _____with rain outside.

j.   The rain falls every day because it is the _____season.

Exercise 3.2b Fill in the blanks with the following.

highest   hottest   warmest   coldest   cooler   hotter   hot   driest   cold

a.   August is the _____ month of the year.

b.   Temperatures are _____ in the month of June than the month of February.

c.   February is the _____ month of the year.

d.   It is _____ in springtime than in summertime.

e.   It is _____ with the air conditioner on.

f.   The earth is getting _____.

g.   It is _____ today. Temperatures are high.

h.   March is the _____ month of all. There is little rain.

i.   It is _____ today. Temperatures are low.

j.   Winter time is freezing. It is the _____ season.

Exercise 3.2c Make five sentences using the comparative and superlative of the words related to weather.

Example: At nighttime the temperatures are cooler than in the day.

1. _____

2. _____

3. _____

4. _____

5. _____

6. _____

Exercise 3.2d Fill in the blanks with the following used as adjective and adverb.

| light | higher | dark | late | early | sunny | clear | on | time |

a. It is getting _____. The sun is rising.

b. It is getting _____. The sun is going down.

c. It is raining. We are not going to get there _____.

d. The wind is blowing. There is a storm coming. We are going to be _____.

e. She gets up _____. She gets up at sunrise.

f. The weather forecast is for _____ days ahead.

g. It is a _____ day. There are no clouds in the sky.

h. I awake at six every morning. I am an _____riser.

i. I stay in bed all morning. I am a _____sleeper.

3.3   Non-Countable and Countable Nouns: Describing the Weather

1. Using *much* and *little*. Some nouns are non-countable. Non-countable nouns are singular.

Example:

money	food	equipment	work
weather	water	furniture	sunshine
rain	wind	news	housework
snow	air	music	information

Little is used with non-countable nouns. *Little* is an adjective of quantity.

Little
There was little rain today.
We have little money in the bank.
There is little snow on the ground.

Much is used with non-countable nouns. *Much* is an adjective of quantity.

Much
There was much rain today.
There was much snow on the mountain.
There was much information on the Internet.

2. Using *few, many, very,* and *a lot*

a. *Few* is used with countable nouns. *Few* is an indefinite adjective.

Few
I had a few dollars in my pocket.
I had a few things.

b. *Many* is used with countable nouns. *Many* is an indefinite adjective.

Many
There were many birds in the trees.
There were many people here yesterday.

c. *Very* is used with *many, much, few,* and *little. Very* is an adverb of degree.

Very	
It was a very hot today.	It was very sunny today.
It is very rainy today.	There is very little rain today.
There are very few people here.	Thank you very much.

d. *A lot* is used with both countable and non-countable nouns.

A lot	
There is a lot of rain today.	There is a lot of snow outside.
There is a lot of sun today.	He has a lot of money.

Note: Common error: It is much hot. It is plenty hot. Correction: It is very hot.

Exercise 3.3a Fill in the blanks with the following.

| many | little | few | very | much |

a.   We have _____ money left in the bank.

b.   There were _____ people in the shops today.

c.   It is _____ hot outside.

d.   There were only a _____ things left to do.

e.   There are _____ children in China.

f.   There were three_____ birds next to the window.

g.   The air is _____ cooler outside.

h.   I had just a _____ dollar in my pocket.

i.   There was _____ rain today.

j.   She has _____ books.

Exercise 3.3b Make simple sentences describing the weather using the following.

much	little	very	a lot

1.   _____

2.   _____

3.   _____

4.   _____

Skills Development
Oral Skills
Q&A

3.4   Student Dialogue

Let's practice using prepositions, adjectives, and adverbs.

Ask your classmate a simple question. Write the answers down.

Student a	What do you do in the evenings ?
Student b	
Student a	What time is your dinnertime?
Student b	
Student a	Do you watch late-night shows on TV?
Student b	
Student a	Do you read the early morning papers?
Student b	
Student a	Do you have late nights out? Do you stay out late?
Student b	
Student a	What time is your English class today?
Student b	

Find the answers to these simple questions.

a.   What time do you get to work?

b.   Are you always late, early or on time?

c.   Would you like to live in a cold country?

d.   Do you get up early?

e. Do you go to bed late?

f. Can you name a winter sport?

g. What is the weather like today?

h. It's summertime! What do you do in summertime?

i. What do you do with your spare time?

j. Do you spend a lot of time on the Internet?

3.5   Expressing Ability and Politeness

Can, Would, Could

1. Using *can*

Can is a means of expressing ability. Very often it is confused with *able to*. *Can* is also used to express permission and politeness and is used often when making requests.

Let's look at some examples.

Expressing ability
We can go shopping.
I can climb a mountain.
I can pass the exam.
I can go out now. The rain has stopped.

Being polite
Can I get you anything?
Can I help you?

Requesting
Can I have the sugar please?
Can we go to the cinema?
Can they enter the show?
Can you tell me how to get to the plaza?
Can you help me please?

The negative *cannot (can't)* expresses inability.

Expressing inability
I cannot pass this exam.
I cannot go to school today because I am ill.
I cannot walk. My feet hurt.
I can't leave now. It is raining.

I can't pass this exam.

Common error: "Can To"
Can is not followed by the preposition *to*.

2. Using *would*

Would as a form of politeness or invitation.

Politeness or Invitation
Would you like some coffee?
Would you like to sit?
Would you like a newspaper?

Note: *Will* can be substituted for *would*.

Would is used when requesting

Requesting
I would like to get some information, please.
Would it be possible to leave early?
Would you buy the groceries later?

Would you like some coffee?

More tea!

3.   Using *could*

Requesting
Could you answer the phone, please?
Could we go to the party?
Could you pass the salt?
Could you tell me how to get to the bank?

Could **is used to express ability.**

Expressing ability
I could speak English.
I couldn't get to the bank. It was raining.

I couldn't get there. It was raining.

> Note: The negative *couldn't* is used in the past tense.

Can, would, **and** *could* **are referred to as modal auxiliaries.**

4.   Using *able to, unable to*

Expressing ability/inability
The plane is able to land. The storm is over.
I am unable to get to school. The weather is bad.
He is unable to get home. The roads are flooded.

Exercise 3.5a Fill in the blanks using *can, can't, able, unable, would,* and *could.*

a.   I _____ get to work. It is snowing heavily.

b.   We _____ go to the park now. It is raining.

c.   She is _____ to walk. Her feet hurt.

d.   They are _____ to buy a house this year. They have the money.

e. I _____ pass this exam. It is too difficult.

f. _____ I get you some coffee?

g. We _____ go out now. It is getting light.

h. _____ you tell me how to get to the bank?

i. The planes _____land at the airport. There is a storm out there.

j. _____ you like some tea?

Exercise 3.5 b Match the following sentences.

a) The rain has stopped.	b) We would never get there on time.
c) It is pouring with rain.	d) Yes, of course.
e) All flights are cancelled.	f) Yes, please. It is very cold today.

1. We can't go to the beach.   _____

2. We can go out now. _____

3. There is much traffic.   _____

4. A hurricane is expected.   _____

5. Could you lend me your umbrella? _____

6. Would you like some hot tea?   _____

Exercise 3.5c Fill in the blanks with the following.

winter   cooler   showers   their   sunny   in   to   at   hot

During the _____, there are many activities taking place in cold climates.

In the state of Colorado, _____ the United States, the sport of skiing is very popular.

Many people go there for _____vacation.

In summer, things are different. The weather is _____ and people spend a lot of time going _____ the beach. Summertime is wonderful. The days are long and the sun goes down _____ nine o'clock. In the tropics, the weather is different. It is _____ all year round.

The months of December and January are, however, _____ months. The rain falls almost every day during the rainy season.

In England, the rain is different. Rains are usually light _____. England has showery spells.

Winters are usually freezing.

Skills Development
Skills Development **Listen and Speak** **Conversation**

3.6   Conversation 7. Expressing Time and Weather

Practice the following conversations with a friend or classmate.

Situation 1. Your friend is arriving from London. You are late, and the weather is bad.

– What time is it?

– It's seven thirty. Look at this storm!

– Yes, I can hear the thunder. We are going to be late. Can you see where you are going?

– No, I can't. The windshield is foggy!

Situation 2. You arrive at the office late. Explain why.

– Good morning. Would you like some coffee?

– Yes, please. Sorry I am late.

– You are soaked! What happened?

– It has been raining all morning. Because of the rain I couldn't get an early bus. Then the traffic was terrible.

– Yes. It's really pouring outside. Here's your coffee.

– Thanks, I really need it.

Traffic

Situation 3. You are at your office, and it is a very hot day. What do you do?

– It is hot today, isn't it?

– Yes, it is even hotter today than yesterday.

– Can you turn the air-conditioning on?

– Sure.

– That's better. I feel cooler already.

Situation 4. Your friend returns from a skiing trip. Ask her about it.

– Tell me about your trip to Colorado. What was the weather like?

– Well, it was snowing when we arrived. It was freezing. At nights we sat by the fire to feel warm.

– Was it fun?

– Oh, yes. We went skiing, and we played in the snow.

– How lovely!

Photo by Steve Nelson

Skills Development
Oral Skills
Q&A

3.7   Student Dialogue

Let's practice using *can, could,* and *would*.

Ask your classmate a simple question. Write the answers down.

Student a	Can you cook?
Student b	
Student a	Can you drive a car?
Student b	
Student a	Can you speak English?
Student b	
Student a	Would you like to be a millionaire?
Student b	
Student a	Would you like to travel all over the world?
Student b	
Student a	Can you sing?
Student b	
Student a	Could you buy a house now?
Student b	

3.8   Outdoor Activities

It's summertime!

Look at the activities. Which ones do you do?

Check them off.

hiking		biking	
river rafting		camping	
car racing		fishing	
diving		hunting	
roller skating		canoeing	
parasailing		swimming	

It's wintertime!

Look at the examples of winter sports. Can you think of any others?

ice hockey	
ice skating	
ice dancing	
bobsled	
figure skating	
luge	
downhill skiing	

3.8a

1.   Make a list of the things people do.

a. during the summer

_____

_____

_____

_____

b. during the winter

_____

_____

_____

_____

Umbrella

Boots

Are you dressed for the weather?

2. Make a list of the things that people wear.

a.   on a hot day

_____   _____

_____   _____

b.   on a rainy day

_____   _____

_____   _____

c.   in wintertime

_____   _____

_____   _____

d)   Make a list of the sporting activities in your country during the summer.

1) _____ 2) _____ 3) _____

4) _____ 5) _____ 6) _____

3.   Describe briefly the weather as it occurs in your country.

_____

_____

_____

_____

3.9   Let's Read: The Geography of Peru

Let's read.

Read the following short passage and answer the questions below.

The Geography of Peru

Peru is a large, mountainous country on the Pacific coast of South America. It borders Ecuador, Colombia, Brazil, Bolivia, Chile, and the Pacific Ocean. The Sierra or mountain region contains the Andes, with peaks of over 6000m (20,000ft). The Selva or forest region is an area of fertile, subtropical uplands, which lies between the Andes and the jungles of eastern Peru. Peru offers much diversity including history, archaeology, sports, beaches, mountains, medicinal springs, nature, fantastic landscapes, friendly people, and music. Tumbes and Piura are the most northerly Peruvian coastal areas and are major beach, surfing, sporting, and deep-sea fishing centres.

Lima is the capital city of Peru. It is an ancient Spanish city founded by Francisco Pizarro in 1535 and known as the "City of Kings." The city's splendid museums, galleries, and monuments are juxtaposed with modern suburbs. Cusco, situated 3360m (11,024ft) above sea level, was once the capital of the Inca Empire. Remains of the granite stone walls of the Inca Palace and temples can still be seen. Peru's most famous archaeological site is Machu Picchu, the "Lost City of the Incas," and the final destination of the famous three-day Inca Trail. Ceviche is a local specialty (uncooked fish marinated in lemon juice and hot pepper, served with corn-on-the-cob, potatoes, and onions). There are many bars, pubs, discotheques, and casinos in the major towns and tourist resorts.

The climate varies according to area. On the coast, winter lasts from June to September. During this period, the mountainous areas are often sunny during the day but cold at night. Heavy rains in the mountains and jungle last from December to April. It never rains in Lima or on most of the coast, except for Tumbes and Piura, which have tropical climates.

Light clothing should be worn during summer. Warmer clothes are needed in upland areas and during the cooler months.[7]

(Source: www.columbusworldtravel.com)

1. Which months of the year are the winter months in Peru?

2. Which months are the rainiest?

3. What do you know about Lima?

4. What do you know about Cusco?

B. Is the weather changing? Is the earth getting hotter?

The future is now!
Read the articles below and answer the questions.
(Source: Weather New Internationalist 319 1999)
www.newint.org

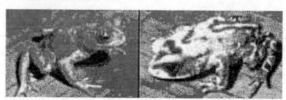

Photo by Tradewind Tours

The Disappearing Toad

The golden toad of Costa Rica has disappeared from the forests. A part of the humid highland forests of Costa Rica, it hasn't been seen for many years. Many scientists believe that the toad has been killed by warmer temperatures caused by global warming. The cloud forest, the habitat of the toad, is drier today than it has been in the past with fewer clouds. The moist, breathing skin of the golden toad was infected as a result of the climate changes. Many other frogs and toads worldwide are also showing deformities of one kind or another, most likely because of rising temperatures and ultraviolet radiation.

Corals Turn White

Corals are losing their color and becoming white as sea temperatures rise and waters become more acidic due to higher carbon-dioxide levels. Coral bleaching can be seen all over the world. Caribbean corals, which help protect coastlines, are endangered, as well as colonies in the Pacific and Indian Oceans. Fish that depend on these corals are dying. In Australia, as the Great Barrier Reef is destroyed, so could the livelihoods of thousands of people who depend on the tourists who visit the country to see the reef.

Photo by Tradewind Tours

1. What does the writer say about the golden toad of Costa Rica?

    _____

    _____

    _____

2. What does the writer say about the corals?

    _____

    _____

    _____

3.10   Introducing the Adverb Clauses of Time

Before, after, while, when, whenever, as, as soon as, until

Let's look at the words that describe time and events.

| before | after | while | when | whenever | as soon as | as | until | since |

- I never saw him <u>before.</u>

- I saw him <u>after</u>.

- Wait a <u>while</u>.

- I have not seen him <u>since</u>.

While I'm waiting, I think I will have a cup of coffee.

To join sentences, use *when, after, before, while, as, whenever, since, until,* and *as soon as* as conjunctions to introduce the adverb clause.

Let's look at the examples.

Examples:

when	
I arrived in Spain. It was raining.	It was raining when I arrived in Spain.

after	
The rain stopped. We went to the city.	We went to the city after the rain stopped.

while	
The rain started falling again. We were shopping in the city.	The rain started falling again while we were shopping in the city.

before	
We left the city. It was getting dark.	We left the city before it got dark.

3.11   Introducing the Adverb Clauses of Cause and Effect

Before   since   now that   as long as

To join sentences, use *because, since, now that,* and *as long as*: conjunctions that introduce the clause.

Let's look at the examples:

now that	
We can leave. The sun is out.	We can leave now that the sun is out.

because	
I am not going to work. There is a storm coming.	I am not going to work because there is a storm coming.

as long as	
We can go anywhere. The weather is fine.	We can go to anywhere as long as the weather is fine.

Since	
We can go to the beach. The weather is fine.	We can go to the beach since the weather is fine.

Skills Development
Listen and Speak

Someone is needed to read the sentences below. Listen to the speaker and repeat the sentences.

a.   It rained every day when I was in France.

    It snowed every day when I was in Chicago.

b.   She went home after the rain stopped.

    She is going to England after she passes her exams.

c.   I am going to leave before it starts raining.

    She wrote her exams before she left for London.

d.   The rain started as I was leaving home.

    As I was leaving the office, the rain stopped.

e.   I carry my raincoat and umbrella whenever it rains.

    Whenever it snows, I wear my boots.

f.   We can go out as soon as the rain stops.

    We can leave as soon as the man comes back.

g.   We can watch the news while we are waiting for him.

    He came home while I was on the phone.

h.   We have not seen him since he left for London.

    The weather has been bad since the rains started in June.

    (Note: *Since* is used with the past participle.)

i.   We stayed until classes were over.

    We waited until the rain stopped.

Now listen to the speaker again.

a.   He decided to wait because it was raining.

He was late for work because it was raining all morning.

b.   He decided to wait since it was raining.

He went to the beach since it was hot.

c.   I can leave now that the rains have stopped.

We can build our house now that we have the money.

d.   We can see everything as long as we have time.

We can go to the beach as long as the weather is fine.

3.12   Conversation 8. Accepting and Refusing Invitations and Expressing Politeness and Ability

Practice the conversations below with a classmate or friend.

You can change the wording and create new conversations.

Situation 1. Accepting an invitation

- We are early! While we are waiting, would you like to go for some coffee?

- Yes, thank you. We can go to the cafe at the corner.

- Fine. We can go as long as it's close by.

Situation 2. Refusing an invitation

- Would you like to go to lunch? There is a great place at the mall.

- Thank you very much, but I can't go. I am sorry. I have an appointment at 12:30.

- Maybe another time?

- Yes, of course. It's because I have an appointment I am unable to go.

- We can go whenever you have the time.

Situation 3. Expressing politeness

- Can I help you?

- Yes, thank you. It is raining so hard it's pouring, and I need to get to my job interview. Whenever it rains, I usually walk with an umbrella but this time I forgot.

- Would you like to borrow mine?

- That would be fine. Thank you very much

- It is nothing. You are welcome.

Situation 4. Expressing ability

- Now that the rain is gone, we can go out.

- Yes. We can go to the park.

– And we can go to the restaurant after for an early dinner.

– Wonderful. Let's go!

Exercise 3.12a Fill in the blank with the suitable words.

| since | Before | because | while | after | before |

a. He left on Thursday. She hasn't seen him _____.

b. We went to the movie. We came home _____.

c. He came home _____ the show ended.

d. He stayed in bed _____ he felt ill.

e. He stayed at home _____ he felt better.

f. It began raining _____ I was waiting for the bus.

g. He got up late. It was _____ 12:00 PM.

h. _____ I was on vacation it rained every day.

i. Please call me _____ dinner.

j. We left early. We left _____ the show ended.

Exercise 3.12b Join the sentences by using the following.

| because | as soon as | whenever | while | when | after | before |

a. She went to bed. She was tired.

b. The storm started. He was waiting to go home.

c. We can go to lunch. We finish the report.

d. I turn the air-conditioning on. It is hot.

e. She went to Paris. She finished university.

f. I was in New York. I saw the plays.

g. She goes away. She is going to sell her house first.

h. I travel to England. I always take my raincoat.

i.   I will travel. I get my passport.

j.   We can leave. He comes back.

Exercise 3.12c Let's practice using *while, before, after, because,* and *whenever.*

Match the sentences.

a) the man walked into the room.   b)   she has to finish high school.
c) the show was cancelled.   d)   she went to bed.
e) I am going on vacation.   f)   I visit my friends.

1.   While she was standing at the door, _____

2.   Before applying for a job, _____

3.   After she finished her homework, _____

4.   Because of the bad weather, _____

5.   As soon as I get my salary, _____

6.   Whenever I am in the city, _____

Exercise 3.12d Let's practice using *when, since, as long as, now that, until,* and *as soon as.*

Match the sentences.

a) he went home.   b)   I saw Buckingham Palace.
c) we can relax.   d)   he can travel.
e) you take care.   f)   you can go.

Note: the comma follows the clause.

1.   When I was in London, _____.

2.   Since he was feeling unwell, _____.

3.   As long as he has a ticket, _____.

4.   Now that exams are over, _____.

5.   As soon as he comes, _____.

6.   Until we meet again, _____.

Exercise 3.12e Fill in the blanks with the following.

as soon as   as long as   now that   until   while

1. She ran to greet me_____ she saw me.

2. _____the game is over, we can go home.

3. She has to stay in bed_____ she gets better.

4. _____he was having dinner, the door bell rang.

5. You can buy it_____ you can pay for it.

6. We waited _____ it got dark.

7. They stayed _____ the sun rose.

8. We are leaving _____ it gets light.

9. We are early. We need to wait a _____.

10. We are late. We need to leave _____possible.

Exercise 3.12f Fill in the blanks.

when   because   as soon as   while   since   whenever

_____I was in Toronto, I saw many interesting things. One day I took a train to Montreal._____was traveling, I met many interesting people. Everyone seemed happy.

_____I arrived in Montreal, the snow started to fall. Until then, the weather was cool with bright sunshine._____I did not have a jacket I felt cold.

_____I travel, I always take a coat and umbrella but this time I forgot. _____ of the weather I returned quickly to Toronto.

Exercise 3.12g Fill in the blanks.

after   before   now   that   whenever   because   as long as

_____ I finished the exam I felt better. It was not difficult at all. _____ the exam I felt nervous and afraid. _____ the exams are over, and it is summertime, I can go to the beach with my friends.

_____ I go to the beach, I always take my suntan oil with me and my sunglasses.

_____ of the hot sun, I need to protect my skin and eyes. I am looking forward to my summer vacation and to spending time with my friends. _____ I have a few good friends, I am happy.

Exercise 3.12h Fill in the blanks.

after before as long as whenever when because as soon as until since

a.   Anyone can have his share _____ he works for it.

b.   Everyone came _____ it was possible to do so.

c.   I saw the man _____ I was looking out the window.

d.   _____ I arrived, many people were already there.

e.   _____ I travel I carry just a few things.

f.   _____ Thursday I haven't seen anyone.

g.   My family and I came late. We came _____ the party ended.

h.   I live on Bolivar Street _____ it is near the university.

i.   _____ I lived in an apartment. Now I live in a house at #10 Sunny Villas.

j.   I waited _____ she came back.

Exercise 3.12i Write sentences using the following as adverb clauses.

after before while whenever when since

3.13   The Future Tense

Table 15: Comparing the present, past, and future tenses

Present	Past	Future
I go to school.	I went to school.	I will go to school.
I do homework.	I did homework.	I will do homework.
I have a car.	I had a car.	I will have a car.

NB/The phrase *going to* is also used to denote the future.

Example:

As soon as I get money, I am going to buy a car.

Exercise 3.13a Identify the tenses in the following sentences.

a.   Tonight after the news I will look at a movie.

b.   Next week I will begin my new job.

c.   Tomorrow I will ask him for my book.

d.   Later I will be going to the disco.

e.   Last night I went to the disco.

f.   I am going out.

g.   He is reading the newspapers.

h.   I had a great time at the party.

i.   I slept all day yesterday.

j.   They will look at a house tomorrow.

Exercise 3.13b Convert the sentences to the future tense.

a.   Yesterday I baked a pie.   _____

b.   I took a vacation last summer.   _____

c.   I went to the shops yesterday.   _____

d.   They bought a new house.   _____

e.   I took my exam last week.   _____

f.   I am looking at television now.   _____

g.   I sent an e-mail to my friend.   _____

h.   I went to school yesterday.   _____

i.   He traveled to New York last month. _____

j.   She cooked dinner last night.   _____

last week	yesterday	last summer	now	last night
next week	tomorrow	next summer	later	tomorrow night
next year	next month	next Monday	last	tonight

Exercise 3.13c Look at the following verbs and the tenses.

Present	Past	Future
send	sent	will send
buy	bought	will buy
go	went	will go
have	had	will have
do	did	will do
speak	spoke	will speak
walk	walked	will walk
give	gave	will give

Construct sentences using the above verbs in all three tenses.

Exercise 3.13d Convert the sentences to the future tense and use a suitable pronoun.

I did my homework yesterday.   I will do it today.

I spoke to Mary.   I will speak with her.

I walked with Andy to school.   _____

He bought Susan a present.   _____

They sent Pablo an e-mail.   _____

She saw Tony yesterday.   _____

I took a message for Cindy.   _____

I gave my sister the money.   _____

I wrote my exam today.   _____

They saw the movie yesterday   _____

She took her brother to the zoo.   _____

Exercise 3.13e . Fill in the blanks using the following.

| after | before | while | whenever | when | as soon as |

a. _____ I get my passport, I will go to New York.

b. _____ I am leaving, I will turn the lights off.

c. _____ I am waiting at the shop, I will telephone the office.

d. I will clean the house _____ they leave it.

e. _____ leaving for New York, I will finish the work.

f. I will lend you the book _____ you need it.

g. _____ we arrive in London, we will take a cab to the hotel.

h. _____ dinner I will call her. I am eating now.

i. _____ I am in London, I will go to the theatre.

j. We will leave _____ possible.

Exercise 3.13f Fill in the blanks using the following.

| now that | since | because | as long as |

a. _____ of the weather we will not be going to the beach.

b. _____ we have money we will buy a bigger house.

c. _____ a storm is expected, all flights will be cancelled.

d. _____ we have love there will always be happiness.

e. _____ he is ill, he will not be going to school.

f. _____ we have no money we will not be buying the car.

g. We will buy a new car _____ we have the money.

h. _____ I am getting paid today I will book a flight.

i. _____ of the rain, I will not be going to the games.

Skills Development
Writing
Describing

3.14   Written Exercises

A. Summertime is the time for fun. Describe, using the past tense, a time you
    spent with friends or family during the summer.

Use the indefinite pronoun, adjectives of quantity, and adverb clauses of
cause and effect and time in your description.

| everyone | much | few | many | good | because | when | best |

Examples: Everyone had a good time. There was much food.

Describe the weather.

_____

_____

_____

_____

_____

B.   Your friend sends you e-mail telling you she plans to visit you for the sum-
     mer. Reply, telling her about the weather and what she will need to wear.

Use the adverb clauses of cause and effect to respond.

_____

_____

_____

_____

C.   Write about some future events you think will happen in your life.

_____

_____

_____

_____

_____

> ## Skills Development
> ## Oral Skills
> ## Role Plays

3.15   Role Play: Dealing with the Situation

a.   A major client is coming in from New York. He asks about the weather. Tell him/her what it is like.

b.   There is a hurricane outside and you cannot get to work. Call and explain why you can't come in.

c.   You need to meet someone to discuss business. Call and invite him/her to dinner.

d.   Invite your friend for coffee.

e.   Your friend invites you to lunch but you are unable to go. What do you say?

f.   You are in a hurry and you need to know the time. Ask someone what time it is.

g.   You need to get some information on courses at the university. Call and find out about the courses.

h.   You are at the gas station and you have a flat tire. Ask for help.

i.   You wish to leave work early. Ask your boss for permission to leave.

j.   Your good friend is visiting your home. Be polite to your friend.

Skills Development
Listen &
Comprehend

Pre-listening task

Let's begin with a look at the vocabulary.

suntan	sunburn
overexposure	UV rays
skin	cancer
allergies	colds
flu	protection
virus	spread
indoor	outdoor

Now let's answer some simple questions. Check the appropriate box.

QUESTION	YES	NO
Can the weather affect your health?		
Can overexposure to the sun affect your skin?		
Can the weather cause a flu outbreak?		
Can you prevent skin cancer from the sun?		
Have you ever had a cold?		

Now let's listen to what the speakers say.

3.16   Scripts 5, 6.

Someone is required to read Scripts 5 and 6. (Appendices 4 and 5). Listen to the speaker and answer the questions below.

A.   Safety in the Sun

Many people need to be educated about the dangers of overexposure to the sun. Listen to following brief report. Answer the questions below.

1) What is the most common form of cancer according to the report?

2) What is the most important factor in the development of skin cancer?

3) What are two things they recommend to protect the skin?

4) Can the sun affect all skin types?

B.   The Common Cold

According to the National Institute of Allergy and Infectious Diseases, almost one billion colds are suffered by people in the United States each year. Listen to what they say about the common cold.

1) What seasons are known to have a high number of people with the common cold?

2) Are colds common among children or adults?

3) How can you prevent a cold?

3.17   Review Exercises

A. Review of *can, can't, could,* and *couldn't.* Fill in the blanks.

1. I _____ go now because the rain is falling.

2. We _____ get to the airport on time because the roads were blocked.

3. They _____ leave whenever they wish.

4. No way! We _____ afford it.

5. I _____ buy the house because I did not have the money.

6. _____ you pass the ketchup please?

7. _____ I see your passport please?

8. She is bright. She _____ surely pass the exam.

9. I _____ walk. My feet hurt.

10. This machine _____ do anything.

B. Write simple sentences using *would* as a polite request.

1. _____

2. _____

3. _____

4. _____

C. Review the comparative and superlative. Fill in the blanks with the appropriate word.

1. It is _____ (cold) today than yesterday.

2. It is _____ (hot) today than yesterday.

3. Turn the air conditioner on. The room will be _____ (cool).

4. July days are _____ (sun) than December days.

5. It is _____ (warm) during the day than at nights.

6. There is much rain today. Yesterday was _____ (dry).

7. Air temperatures are _____ (low) on the mountains.

8. We had much _____ sun yesterday than today (more/most)

9. Yesterday was the _____ snow we have had in a long time (more/most)

D. Join the sentences below using *when, while, after, before,* and *until.*

Use any combination you wish. Underline the clauses.

1. I got a train to London finally. I waited a long time at the station.

2. I took a course in Spanish. I went to Panama.

3. I arrived in Lima. It was freezing.

4. I was sitting at the bar. I met a wonderful person.

5. We stood under the bridge. The rain stopped.

6. I was in Paris. I saw the museums.

7. I arrived at the office. He was already waiting.

8. We closed the deal. We went to dinner.

9. She studies late at nights. Everyone has gone to bed.

10. I waited at the hospital. I was sure everything was fine.

E. Join the sentences below using *because, since, now that,* and *as long as.*
    Underline the clauses.

Note: One conjunctive word can be used in many of these cases.

1. We can't get to the airport. The roads are blocked with fallen trees.

2. We can't get to the park. It is raining.

3. He can leave on time. The roads are cleared.

4. He hasn't eaten dinner. His cat died last Friday.

5. We can rent a car. We have money.

6. I can run a mile. I am fit.

7. We can fix the house. We have the money.

8. He stayed in bed all day. He is not feeling well.

9. He can't walk. He twisted his ankle.

10. We can't get to the meeting. There is a storm out there.

F. Review *much, many, few, a lot,* and *very little.* Fill in the blanks.

1. There are _____ rainy days in the month of June.

2. There is _____ rain in the month of June.

3. It is _____ rainy in the month of June.

4. It is _____ hot today.

5. There is _____ of snow on the ground.

6. He has _____ money in the bank.

7. They have just a _____ dollars left.

8. He is _____ rich.

9. He has a _____ items in his house.

10. He has _____ friends.

CHAPTER 4

📖 **Around: Requesting and Giving Information**

📖 **Locating People, Things, Places**
Prepositions: *Next to, Near*
Adjective Clauses: *When, Where*

4.0   Identifying the Neighborhood

A. Identify the following in the picture above by placing a number next to it.

Description	No.	Description	No.
traffic light		the corner	
sidewalk		street crossing	
mail box		parking meter	
bus stop		the taxi stand	
telephone booth		street lights	

B. Identify the sign by placing a letter next to it. See below.

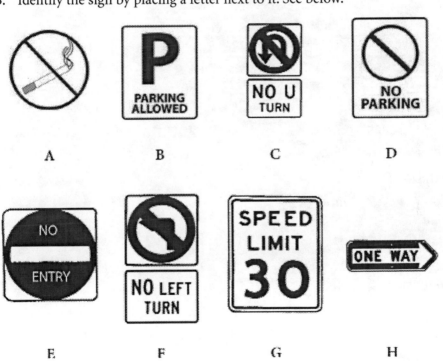

A B C D

E F G H

	Speed Limit 30 mph		One way
	No Entry		No Parking
	No Left Turn		Parking
	No U Turn		No Smoking

Vocabulary

highway	street	enter
motorway	road	stop
miles	traffic	occupied
corner	building	exit
bridge	avenue	vacant
traffic light	avenue	disabled
block	path	entrance
motorcar	subway	closed
line	number	go
station	car park	slow
emergency	open	

Ordinals

first	second
third	fourth
fifth	sixth
seventh	eight
ninth	tenth

Some useful verbs

to turn

to cross

to walk

to drive

to continue

to stop

to pass
to look for
to know
to go
to say/tell

4.1   Asking for and Giving Directions

There are many ways to ask for directions. Let's look at them.

A. Using *would*

Would like
Excuse me, please. I would like to get to the bank.

B. Using *could*

Could you?
Pardon me. Could you show me where the taxi stand is?

C. Using *can*

Can I
Excuse me, please. How can I get to the bank?

Can you tell me how to get to the plaza?

D. Using *where*

Where Is
Pardon me, where is the nearest cafe?

Key words and phrases: (For Spanish students)

English	Spanish
To the left	A la izquierda
To the right	A la derecha
Straight ahead	Todo derecho
Up the street	Calle arriba
Down the street	Calle abajo
At the corner	A la esquina

4.2   Locating People, Things, Places
Some Commonly Used Prepositions

Let's look at the prepositions below. They are commonly used when giving directions.

near to	next to	in front of	behind
at the side of	opposite to	along	through

Look at the sentences below and identify the prepositions in them. (Refer to sketch on page 183)

a.   The man is standing near the mailbox.

b.   He is standing at the corner.

c.   The woman is crossing the street. She is next to the man.

d.   They are in front of the building.

e.   The taxi stand is at the side of the building.

Some important landmarks

bank	restaurant	avenue
the zoo	the palace	plaza
ATM machine	hotel	park
cathedral	church	Internet cafe
museum	mall	hospital
beach	airport	marina

4.3 How Can You Get There?

by subway	by car	on foot
by taxi	by train	by bus
by plane	by boat	by canoe

How can I get to the.......?	Para ir a........?
The sign for the........	La indicador para .....
Can I go....... by bus?	Se puede ir -----en autobus
No, you cannot	No se puede.
through, along	por
around here	por aqui
please	por favor
through the street	por la calle
You can pass along here.	Se puede pasar por aqui.

4.4   Student Dialogue

Let's find out about your town.

Ask your classmate a simple question. Write the answers down.

Student a	Can you tell me how to get to the Internet cafe?
Student b	
Student a	Could you tell me where the bus stop is? How far is it?
Student b	
Student a	Could you tell me how to get to the mall?
Student b	
Student a	I need to get to the airport quickly. Where can I phone a taxi?
Student b	
Student a	How do you get around the city? On foot? By taxi?
Student b	
Student a	What is in front of your house?
Student b	
Student a	What is opposite to the school?
Student b	
Student a	What is at the side of your school?
Student b	
Student a	How far is it to the museum?
Student b	

> **Skills Development**
> **Requesting and Giving**
> **Information**
> **Directions**

4.5   Conversation 9. Asking for Directions

First, let's look at the sketch below.

Sylvia Anderson is visiting the city of Port of Spain and needs to get around.

Read the conversations below and follow the directions. Repeat the dialogue with your friend.

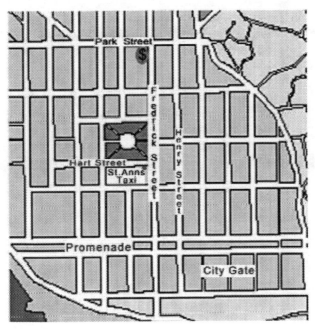

Situation 1.

At the moment she is at City Gate and wants to do some shopping.

- Excuse me, please. Can you tell me how to get to the main shopping area?
- You need to go downtown. Cross the promenade at the traffic light and continue along Henry Street. Turn left onto Frederick Street.
- Thank you.
- You are welcome.

Situation 2.

She decides to buy more items. She needs to exchange money.

- Excuse me, please. Where is the nearest bank?
- The nearest bank is at the corner of Frederick and Park Street.
- How can I get there?
- You can walk there. Just continue straight along Frederick Street until you get to the corner. Take a right turn, and you will find it.
- Thanks.
- Okay, bye.

Situation 3.

She completes her shopping and wants to return to her hotel. She is staying at Pelican Hotel in St. Ann's.

- Hello. Can you tell me how to get to the Pelican Hotel?
- You need a taxi to get there. You can get a taxi at Hart Street.
- How far is it?
- It is near. Continue walking up Frederick Street. Cross at the first traffic light, and you will find it.
- Thank you.
- You are welcome.

Exercise 4.5a Look at the sketch below. Sylvia is now standing on Colville Street. She wishes to get to the following areas. Can you direct her?

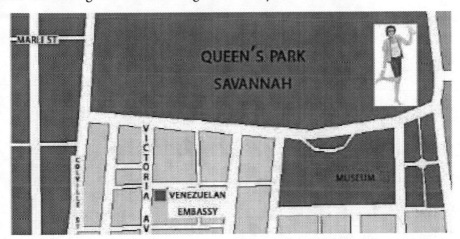

1. Queen's Park Savannah

    _____

    _____

    _____

    _____

2. National Museum

    _____

    _____

    _____

    _____

3. Venezuelan Embassy on Victoria Avenue at #10

    _____

    _____

    _____

    _____

4. The Internet cafe on Mali Street

_____

_____

_____

_____

Exercise 4.5b Fill in the blanks.

near to | next to | at the side of | in front of | cross | on foot | with | at

I love my city. It has everything I need. _____ _____ _____ _____ my apartment there is an Internet cafe. _____ _____ the Internet cafe is a very good restaurant.

The food is excellent. I go everywhere _____ _____.

I do not need to take a taxi or a bus. On Saturdays I spend a lot of time walking around the city.

Not very far away or _____ _____ my apartment there is a mall.

I have lunch there _____ my friend Alberta. Usually we meet _____ 11.30 AM _____ _____ _____ the shoe shop in the mall. My friend Alberta is very nice.

She is a university student and she studies engineering. After lunch we _____ the avenue and go to cinema which is _____ _____ _____ the disco.

**Skills Development
Oral Skills
Conversation**

**4.6   Conversation 10. Getting around the
neighborhood**

4.6.1   At the Bank

Requesting and giving information

Situation 1.

Practice the conversations below with a friend or classmate.

– Hi, Juan. How are you?

– Fine, thank you, Carlos. I need to get to a bank. Can you tell me where it is?

– The bank is at the end of the street at the corner. I am going there now. Let's go.

– I need to open an account. I have to deposit money.

– To open an account you need to have personal ID.

– I have my passport. Will that be okay?

– That's fine.

Situation 2

Meeting the bank clerk and opening an account

Bank clerk	-	Good morning. How can I help you?
Carlos	-	I would like to open a bank account.
Bank clerk	-	What type of account?
Carlos	-	A savings account.
Bank clerk	-	No problem. I need to see some identification. Do you have a passport?
Carlos	-	Yes, I do. Here it is.
Bank clerk	-	You need to sign these forms. And how much do you wish to deposit?
Carlos	-	Five thousand dollars.
Bank clerk	-	Okay. One moment. Here's your bankbook and ATM card. Have a nice day.
Carlos	-	Thank you. Bye

Key words

Translate into your language.

deposit

percent

savings account

checking account

bank account

ATM machine

password

bank book

passport

identification

to sign

signature

forms

deposit slip

withdrawal slip

The World Currencies and Major Languages

Country	Currency	Major Language
Argentine	Peso	Spanish
Australia	Australian Dollar	English
Brazil	Cruzeiro	Portuguese
Canada	Canadian Dollar	English, French
China	Yuan	Chinese (Mandarin)

Country	Currency	Major Language
Hong Kong	Hong Kong Dollar	English, Chinese (Cantonese, Mandarin)
India	Rupee	Hindi, English, Bengali, Bihari, Marathi
Japan	Yen	Japanese
Korea (North)	Won	Korean
Mexico	Mexican Nuevo Peso	Spanish, Amerindian
Russia	Ruble	Russian
Sweden	Swedish	Swedish Krona
United Kingdom	Pound Sterling	English, Welsh, Gaelic
Venezuela	Bolivar	Spanish, Amerindian

More key words

rules
bank manager
bank
bank clerk
counter
at any time
customer
foreign exchange

to change a check
interest on loan (e.g. 5%, 8%)
to come back/ to return
client
loan/ to borrow
to save
easy payments plan
installment
monthly installments
cash
loan plans

Mr. Brown Buys a Car

Look at the item below. Mr. Joe Brown is a teacher, and he wishes to purchase the car but he doesn't have cash. He goes to the bank for a loan.

Fill in the blanks in the conversation below.

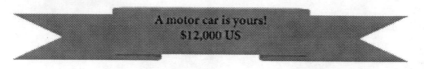

A motor car is yours!
$12,000 US

$12,000 US
$ 300.00 mthly
installment
10% Deposit.

Bank clerk	-	Good morning. How can I help you?
Mr. Brown	-	_____
Bank clerk	-	What is the cost of the item?
Mr. Brown	-	_____
Bank clerk	-	Do you have a job?
Mr. Brown	-	_____
Bank clerk	-	What do you do?
Mr. Brown	-	_____
Bank clerk	-	You need to deposit ten percent of the cost.
Mr. Brown	-	If I pay the ten percent I can get the loan?
Bank clerk	-	Yes.
Mr. Brown	-	And the installments?
Bank clerk	-	_____
Mr. Brown	-	Thanks. I am going to buy the car.

Let's Go Shopping!

4.6.2   Conversation 11. At the Clothes Shop

Requesting and giving information

Practice the following conversation with a classmate or friend.

- Hello. I am looking for a new blouse. Can you help me?

- Yes, of course. Come this way. What kind of blouse are you looking for?

- I would like to buy a red silk blouse of medium size.

- We have those. The cost is ten dollars.

- That is too expensive. Do you have anything less expensive?

- Yes, but not silk. It is cotton.

- That is fine.

- Are you paying by cash, check, or by credit card?

- Credit card. Visa.

- You can pay at the counter.

- Thank you.

- You are welcome.

Exercise 4.6a Identify the items below and translate.

a blouse		a jacket	
a skirt		a shirt	
a pair of shorts		a pair of pants	
underwear		handbags	
a dress		T-shirt	
ties		socks	
belts		jeans	
bathing suit		sweaters	
suit		hats	

Exercise 4.6b Describing the item

Color

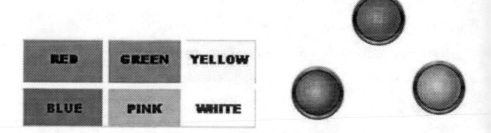

RED	GREEN	YELLOW
BLUE	PINK	WHITE

Type

silk	cotton	polyester	linen	suede	denim	leather

Size

Size of clothes

5	8	10	14
small	med	large	

Paying for the item

| cash | credit card | check |

Match the nouns and adjectives. Choose your favorite color, type, and your size.

Nouns	Adjectives		
	Color	Type	Size
shirt			
pants			
jacket			
bag			
shoes			
caps/hats			
T-shirts			
shorts			

4.6.3   Conversation 12. At the Shoe Shop

Requesting and giving information

Practice the following conversation with a classmate or friend.

- Good morning. Can I help you?

- Yes, I would like to get a pair of tan sandals.

- What size do you wear?

- I wear size five. I have small feet.

- Come this way. Here, try these on.

- These are perfect. How much?

- Fifty dollars.

- Okay, I will take them.

Vocabulary skills

Some key words and phrases

Translate into your language.

It suits you.		flat shoes	
It fits you well.		high heels	
It is comfortable.		sports wear	
It is too tight.		shopping spree	
It is too small.		items	
It is big.		salesperson	
to shop		damaged items	
to buy		good buys	
to spend		returned items	

4.6.4   Conversation 13. At the Grocery

Requesting and giving information

Practice the following conversation with a friend or classmate.

Student a	How can I help you?
Student b	I would like to get a pound of beef, please.
Student a	Do you need anything else?
Student b	Yes. Can I get a pound of bananas as well, please?
Student a	Will that be all?
Student b	Yes, thank you.

Student a	Ten dollars, please.
Student b	Here's the money. Keep the change.
Student a	Thank you.

Translate the items below into your language.

corn		meat	
ham		butter	
bananas		milk	
sweet potato		fish	
apples		shrimp	
plums		soda	
pawpaw		water	
grapes		coffee	
tuna		chicken	
salmon		rice	
macaroni		fruit	
potato		sugar	
vegetable		salt	
cheese		bread	
tea		carrots	
celery		onion	

Exercise 4.6c Creating an ad.

Look at the ads below.

a)   List the items that you see.   b)   What do the ads tell us?

_____   _____

_____   _____

_____   _____

_____   _____

_____   _____

Now create your own ad. List three items you are selling and the cost of the items.

Skills Development
Grammar& Exercises

4.7   Using the Adverb *Where* in an Adjective Clause

An adjective clause can be introduced by a relative/conjunctive adverb or a relative pronoun.

Consider the following sentences. *Where* is used as the adjective clause. It refers to the antecedent noun.

1.   The Grand Mall is in the city. She shops there.

     The Grand Mall in the city is <u>where she shops</u>.

2.   The meat shop is at the corner. She buys meat there.

     The meat shop at the corner is <u>where she buys her meat.</u>

Exercise 4.7a Join the following sentences using *where* in the relative clause.

a.   The new pharmacy. She buys her medicine there.

b.   The old shoe shop. She buys her sneakers there.

c.   The blue house on the hill. He lives there.

d.   This is the great country. They came from there.

e.   The new building. He works there.

f.   The big bank. He has an account there.

g.   The bright city of Las Vegas. They live there.

h.   The village market. She buys her vegetables there.

i.   The expensive clothes shop at the mall. She shops there.

4.8   Using the Adverb *When* as an Adjective Clause

When is used as the adjective clause to describe time. *When* is used to join sentences.

Examples:

July the fourth is the day. We celebrate Independence Day (on that day).

July the fourth is the day <u>when we celebrate Independence Day</u>.

Exercise 4.8a Join the following sentences using *when*.

a)   Christmas is a time of the year. We buy gifts for our loved ones.

b)   Monday is the fifth. We will have our final exams.

c)   Sunday is the day. I go to church (on that day).

d)   I will never forget the day. We got married (on that day).

e)   2001 was the year. We celebrated our second anniversary.

f)   1:00 PM is the time. They will arrive from Boston.

g)   August is the month. The weather is usually the hottest.

h)   1996 was the year. I began university.

i)   Tuesday is the day. We have gym classes.

4.9   Noun Clauses

The question words *when, why, where, how, whose,* and *which* are used to introduce the noun clause.

A noun clause is used as a subject or an object.

Examples:

Let's look at some questions.

1. Where does your mother shop? Do you know?

2. What does she like? Do you know?

3. How old is she?

4. Whose car is it? Do you know?

5. When are they coming back from their trip?

6. Which one does he want? Do you know?

7. What did he say?

Let's look at some answers.

1. The New City Mall at the corner is <u>where she shops</u>.

    This is an adjective clause.

2. I don't know <u>how old she is</u>.

3. I don't know <u>whose car it is.</u>

4. I don't know <u>when they are coming back from their trip.</u>

5. I don't know <u>which one he wants.</u>

6. I don't know <u>what he said.</u>

The underlined words in sentences 2–6 are noun clauses.

Let's find the answers to some more questions!

Q. How much did you pay for the car? Can you remember?

A. _____

Q. How many people live in your country? Do you know?

A. _____

Q. Who is the prime minister of England?

A. _____

Q. What is the capital of China?

A. _____

Q. Where is the nearest doctor's office?

A. _____

Q. Which city in the world is famous for fast foods?

A. _____

Q. Whose house is the most expensive in the world?

A. _____

Skills Development
Oral Skills
Q&A

4.10   Student Dialogue

Who?   What?   When?   Where?   How?   Which?

Find the answers to these simple questions.

Student a	What do people wear to the beach?
Student b	
Student a	What do people wear to the office?
Student b	
Student a	Where does your mother shop?
Student b	
Student a	What are the things she likes to buy?
Student b	
Student a	Which is her favorite shopping day?
Student b	
Student a	How much money does she spend?
Student b	
Student a	When do you shop most?
Student b	

Skills Development
Oral Skills
Role Plays

4.11   Role Play: Dealing with the Situation

a.   Your friend wishes to go to the nearest cafe for coffee. Tell her where to go.

b.   A tourist wishes to exchange money. What do you tell him/her?

c.   You get a call from your friend who is at the airport. Tell him/her how to get to your home.

d.   You lose your bank card and credit card. What do you do?

e.   You need information about a money transfer. Ask the bank clerk to help you.

f.   You are in a foreign country and you don't know the bank hours. Ask someone.

g.   You are a salesperson in a store. Greet the customer and find out what he wants.

h.   Your friend wants to buy a child's dress. Tell her what to do.

i.   You buy a pair of shoes but they do not fit well. Take them back and ask the salesperson for a new one.

j.   You need to get apples and grapes at the fruit mart. Ask for the items, and find out how much each item costs.

Skills Development
Reading
Comprehension

4.12   Let's Read

The Internet Reborn

The current Internet is outdated. Read and find out what's in the future for the Internet.

Global ambitions: Princeton University's Larry Peterson wants to make the Internet's Infrastructure more intelligent.
(Photograph by Beth Perkins)

A grassroots group of leading computer scientists, backed by Intel and other heavyweight industrial sponsors, is working on replacing today's Internet with a faster, more secure, and vastly smarter network.

By Wade Roush—October 2003

If you're like most cyber-citizens, you use the Internet for e-mail, Web searching, chatting with friends, music downloads, and buying books and gifts. More than 600 million people use these services worldwide—far more than anyone could have predicted in the 1970s, when the Internet's key components were conceived. An estimated $3.9 trillion in business transactions will take place over the Internet in 2003, and the medium's reach is increasingly global: an astonishing 24 percent of Brazilians, 30 percent of Chinese, and 72 percent of Americans now go online at least once per month.

Still, despite its enormous impact, today's Internet is like a 1973 Buick refitted with air bags and emissions controls. Its decades-old infrastructure has been rigged out with the Web and all it enables (like e-commerce), plus technologies such as streaming media, peer-to-peer file sharing, and videoconferencing; but it's still a 1973 Buick. Now, a grassroots group of nearly 100 leading computer scientists, backed by heavyweight industrial sponsors, is working on replacing it with a new, vastly smarter model.[9]

1) According to the article, how many people worldwide use the Internet?

2) How many Brazilians use the Internet?

3) How many Americans use the Internet?

4) What are the scientists trying to do?

Skills Development
Writing

4.13   Written Exercises

1. Write one paragraph describing your neighborhood.
    Use prepositions to locate important landmarks.

    _____

    _____

    _____

2. Write one paragraph describing the activities in your neighborhood.
    Use *when* and *where* as adjective clauses.

    _____

    _____

    _____

3. Write an e-mail to your friend describing the great sales that are on. Invite
    her/him to go shopping with you.
    Use the noun clause (e.g., *I don't know what you like*, etc).

    _____

    _____

    _____

4. You are going to the grocery to do your weekend shopping. Make a list of
    the things you need to buy.

Skills Development
Listen and
Comprehend

Pre-listening task:

First let's look at the vocabulary.

Vocabulary

communications	computer	translator
device	technology	download
message	e-book	technologist
automatic	machine	video
Internet	e-mail	cell phone

Now let's answer some simple questions about the future.

Do you think that in the future…(Check the appropriate box.)

QUESTION	YES	NO
The Internet will be everywhere?		
Machines will translate and speak any language?		
We will be to communicate with people with screens as in the movie *Star Trek*?		
Cell phones and computers will be so tiny they can fit in your pocket?		
The refrigerator will make a grocery list and order items online?		

4.14   Script 7. The Future of Communications

Someone is required to read script 7 (appendix 6). Listen to the speaker and answer the questions below.

1)   What does he say about cell phones?

2) What does he say about e-books?

3) What does he say about languages?

4.15   Review Exercises

A.   Fill in the blanks with the past tense.

1.   She _____ (to buy) several items at the mall on Sunday.

2.   She _____ (to pay) ten dollars for her shirt at the grand sale.

3.   He _____ (to ask) for ten pounds of beef at the meat shop.

4.   They _____ (to go) to the bank to get a loan.

5.   He _____ (to open) a saving account at the City Bank.

6.   He _____ (to spend) all his money at the Internet cafe.

7.   They _____ (to shop) everyday during their vacation.

8.   The black suit _____ (to fit) him well.

9.   He _____ (to change) money at the bank.

10.   We _____ (to visit) the museum in the city.

B.   Fill in the blanks with the past continuous.

1.   She _____ (to buy) items at the mall when the fire alarm went off.

2.   He _____ (to pay) for his pants at the counter when he met her.

3.   He _____ (to ask) for ten pounds of beef when his friend came in.

4.   They _____ (to go) to the bank when the rain started.

5.   He _____ (to open) an account at the City Bank when the robber appeared.

6.   She _____ (to try) on a jacket when her friend came into the store.

7.   While he _____ (to wait) for a taxi, his friend came by.

8.   She _____ (to walk) along the main plaza when the rain started.

9.   He _____ (to run) along the grassy field when he slipped.

10.   He _____ (to exercise) at the gym when he got the call.

C. Sentence conversion. Convert the sentences into one.

Use *who, which, that, when, where, what, whom,* and *whose* (the relative clauses).

1. I thanked the shop attendant. She was very helpful to me.

2. The jacket was very expensive. I liked it.

3. The manager is sitting in the room. I met him on Saturday.

4. Today is the day. They will come.

5. The blue house. She lives there.

6. I saw the car. It was not good.

7. It was interesting. He said it.

8. The man is sitting there. I live in his house.

9. Thursday is the day. I go to the gym.

10. The new office building at the corner. She works there.

D. Fill in the blanks with the following:

When, whenever, as soon as, while, as, until, before, and *after*

1. _____ I go to the bank I take my bank card with me.

2. I waited _____ the bank opened.

3. _____ I passed the mall, I saw the ads.

4. _____I arrived, the bank was already closed.

5. ____ _____ _____ I get money I am going shopping.

6. You better get to the bank _____ it closes!

7. _____ the holiday we can go back to work.

8. _____I was waiting for her at the bank, the lights went off.

9. We will be able to buy fresh vegetables everyday ____ _____ ____ the new mart opens across the street.

10. _____ I feel ill. I stay at home.

E. Fill in the blanks with the following.

Because, since, as long as, and *now that*

1. _____ it is a holiday the shops are closed.

2. _____ you have money you can buy anything.

3. _____ the groceries are shut I can't buy anything today.

4. _____ you have a job you can buy a car.

5. _____ it is summertime, the sales are on.

6. _____ the shops and banks are next to each other, we can do everything faster.

7. We can finish our Christmas shopping _____ the shops close late.

8. _____ the school is near my house, I always get to school on time.

9. _____ there is a new Internet cafe opposite my home, I can send e-mail anytime.

Note: *since* and *because* are the same in these cases, as are *as* and *while.*

F. Fill the blanks using the following.

Few, many, little, much, any, some, and *all*

1. He has_____ money in the bank. He cannot buy the car.

2. She has a _____ dollars to buy groceries.

3. I didn't buy _____ meat in the meat shop. I bought vegetables instead.

4. I need to get _____ flour. I am going to the grocery.

5. I don't have _____ time left.

6. The shops are _____ closed.

7. _____ the students are at home.

8. _____ the banks charge interest.

9. There are _____ banks in my neighborhood.

10. _____of the banks are closed at 2:00 PM. In fact, almost _____of them are closed.

G. Fill in the blanks with the positive, comparative and superlative.

Better, more expensive, more beautiful, best, cheaper, and *tighter*

1. My old computer is good but I need a _____one.

2. The green jacket is _____than the gray.

3. The new shop sells the _____ pants.

4. You can get _____prices at the market.

5. Your dress beautiful. It is _____than mine.

6. The pair of shoes does not fit. It is _____ than the sneakers.

7. The new clothes shop at the end of the street is the _____ one.

8. You can get _____prices next door.

9. The meat shop at the corner is not cheap. It is _____than the one nearby.

10. At the side of the bank you can find the _____restaurant.

H. Let's practice the adverbs and adjectives again.

Late, early, hurriedly, quickly, fast, neatly, slowly, and *quick*

1. I am working until ten o'clock. I am going to be _____. Don't wait for me.

2. I want to be there as soon as possible. I am arriving in Miami _____.

3. He took the _____night train home after work.

4. He ran _____ to catch the bus before it left.

5. She took the _____train to New York City. She didn't want to be _____.

6. While he was waiting for her, he read the newspapers _____.

7. He dressed_____ for his job interview.

8. Her feet hurt terribly. She walked _____ to her car.

9. He took a _____ bath. He was in a hurry.

10. She had an _____ dinner. She was hungry.

I. Review the prepositions *for* and *to*. Complete the following.

1. I am going_____ the mall.

2. I like going_____ a walk.

3. Can you take this_____ the bank?

4. I am leaving this_____ her.

5. Can we go_____ the grocery?

6. Who are you waiting_____?

7. Where are you going_____?

8. Can you take this_____them as soon as possible?

9. While I was waiting_____her, I heard the siren.

Skills Development
Pronunciation
Listen and Speak

4.16.   Pronunciation

4.16.1   Pronunciation of the -ed words.

—ed words have -id and -t sounds

Let's practice some words.

words	ending sound
planted	/id (*ted* and *ded* endings follow the /id sound)
ended	/id
walked	/t
stopped	/t
helped	/t
used	/d
stayed	/d

Now repeat the pronunciation of the following.

visited	decided	wanted
lasted	arrived	welcomed
showed	boiled	looked
watched	hoped	crashed

4.16.2.   Pronunciation of the -es and -s words

-s and -es word have/z and/iz sounds

Let's look at some examples

word	ending sound
sells	/z
fishes	/iz
lives	/z
walks	/s
washes	/iz

Possessives adjectives and nouns also have a/z sound

Let's look at some examples.

His/hers/theirs   /z

Jane's pen   /z

Andy's house   /z

Please note -*is* is pronounced -*iz*, not as *eez*.

Now repeat the following words that also have/z sounds.

matches	watches	searches	houses	/z
talks	barks	sparks	speaks	/s
bells	slippers	shoes	tells	/z

4.16.3   The Silent *w*

A *w* before *r* and *h* is silent.

wrong	Wright	whole	write	writer

These are more difficult *w* words. Your teacher will assist you.

won (as one)	wood	wool	world	would

4.16.4   The Silent *r*

	sound
are	(ah)
aren't	(ant)
hair	(as here)

Here are some more difficult words. Your teacher will assist you.

ship	sheep	chip	cheap
hill	heel	will	wheel

Let's practice again.

Listen to the teacher and repeat.

A) *-ed*

-ed sounding *-id*

1.   The woman shouted at the top of her voice.

2.   The flight departed at six.

3.   The plane landed at ten in the morning.

4.   He wanted to see Egypt.

5.   She needed a rest.

6.   They started their journey to Jamaica at 5:00 AM.

7.   The restaurant was crowded at lunchtime.

8.   We visited many places in Cairo.

-ed sounding *-d*

1.   We arrived in Egypt at 4:00 AM.

2.   We talked about the trip for months.

3.   We enjoyed our trip to Egypt.

4.   He carried my luggage to my room.

5. We tried the food in Jamaica. It was wonderful.

6. We used all our money on the trip.

7. We stayed at the best hotel in Paris. We stayed at the Hotel Paris.

8. We traveled everywhere.

-ed sounding *-t*

1. We stopped at the gas station for gas.

2. He helped us with everything.

3. I asked the porter for help.

4. We watched the Nile River from the boat.

5. He pushed his luggage all the way to the counter.

6. He looked tired.

7. We dressed formally for dinner on the Nile.

B) *-es* sounding *-iz*

1. The fishes looked spectacular in the sea.

2. There were many friendly faces on our trip.

3. The games were played on Sunday.

4. We brought boxes of stuff.

5. The houses are very strange.

6. He watches everything carefully.

7. The book has many pages.

C) *-s* and *-es* sounding *-z*

1. He lives alone.

2. His shoes are dirty.

3. The school bells are ringing.

4.   There are many bags on the table.

5.   She tells him everything.

6.   She is wearing slippers.

7.   There are seven days in the week.

D)   *-s sounding -s*

1.   He speaks well.

2.   The students are happy.

3.   He sleeps a lot.

4.   The dog barks all night.

5.   He hates his job.

6.   She likes her job.

7.   The nights are quiet.

(There is a common error with words beginning with s (e.g.,. *special, speak,* and *Spanish*). These words are often incorrectly pronounced as *es school* or *es speak*. There is no *es* before these words! *Soap* and *Soup:* one is a toiletry and one is food.)

E)   *-w* words

1.   The sweater is made of wool.

2.   I would like you to stay.

3.   The writer is very good.

4.   He won the prize.

5.   The world is big.

6.   The table is made of wood.

7.   The car has wheels.

APPENDIX 1

Script 2. Chapter 1
The Life of Sir Isaac Newton

The famous English physicist and mathematician Sir Isaac Newton was one of the greatest scientists of all time.

His theories revolutionized scientific thinking and laid the foundation of today's modern physics. His greatest publication, *Principia Mathematica,* is one of the most important works in the history of modern science.

Sir Isaac Newton was born in Woolsthorpe, near Grantham in Lincolnshire. According to the Gregorian Calendar, he was born on January 4, 1643. He came from a family of farmers, but he never knew his father who died three months before he was born. He did not have a happy childhood. Newton entered Trinity College on June 5, 1661 and became Lucasian professor in 1669 at the age of only twenty-seven. He left Cambridge to become Warden of the Royal Mint in 1696 and Master in 1699. In 1703 he was elected president of the Royal Society. He died on March 31, 1727, in London, England.

Author unknown

APPENDIX 2

Script 3. Chapter 2
An Office Plan

We have a wonderful plan for your office. First you will see the reception area when you enter the front door. To the left of the reception area is the main office. It is the director's office. To the right of the reception area is the secretary's office. Next to each will of course be the private toilets, men's and women's. At the end of the reception area you will find the kitchen, which, by the way, is very spacious and comfortable. Next to the kitchen you will find the storage room. This is a much smaller room and is used for storing files and other documents. Left of the kitchen is the accountant's office. This office is smaller than the director's office. Wonderful! Isn't it?

APPENDIX 3

Script 4. Chapter 2
A House Plan

Hi. Welcome to Orville Home Construction Company. And this is what we have for you!

Just look at the plans, and we will explain. Your house consists of two floors, a first floor and a second floor. The ground floor has a large laundry area at the far end and of course, a beautifully tiled kitchen is next to it. As you enter your house, you will see the living room and dining room. As you pass along the corridor, you will come to the study area and powder room.

As you enter the second floor, you will find the master bedroom, which has a private bathroom. Further along you will find two more bedrooms, each with a private bathroom. These of course are smaller than the master bedroom. All of this at a price of just $150,000 US dollars. Marvelous!

Come in and see us or call 1-800-456-761.

APPENDIX 4

Script 5. Chapter 3
Safety in the Sun

Overexposure to the sun's rays affects people of all ages and skin types throughout the year. Believe it or not, skin cancer is the most common of all cancers, and UV radiation is the most important factor in the development of skin cancer. Before you head outdoors, find out what you can do to protect yourself.

You should wear a wide-brimmed hat and always generously apply a sunscreen that blocks out the UV rays.

Reapply sunscreen after swimming to make sure you are always protected. Waterproof sunscreen can come off when you dry your skin with a towel. People with a high number of moles or freckles should take extra precaution.

Author unknown

APPENDIX 5

Script 6. Chapter 3
Colds and Flu

According to the National Institute of Allergy and Infectious Diseases, people in the United States suffer from almost one billion colds each year. Colds are most common among children. Children have six to ten colds per year. Adults have about two to four colds each year. In the United States, most colds occur in the fall and winter seasons. Beginning in late August or early September, the number of colds increases slowly and remains high until March or April. During these months most people are indoors for long periods of time, increasing the chances of spreading the virus. The dryness of the cold winter months may also be a factor in the spread of the common cold. Hand washing regularly is one of the simplest ways of preventing a cold. It is also important to avoid close contact with people with colds and to avoid touching the nose and the eyes.

Source: USNIAID office of communications and public liaison, USA, 1999

APPENDIX 6

Script 7. Chapter 4
The Future of Communications

We're in for the communications ride of our lives. The coming year will see cell phones small enough to hide in your pocket—really! And small enough to take anywhere in the world.

There will be tiny hand-size computers that know your favorite subjects, and Internet will be everywhere.

Technologists believe 2000 will be the year of video messaging. You will be able to see whom you're talking to. It may be just five years before we can chat on giant screens like *Star Trek's* Captain Kirk. "Kirk Out."

In the next five years, cell phones will sense their locations and feed you information about where you are.

You can't speak the language? In another year or two, that will be no problem.

Oakland police officer Tam Dinh tests a new automatic translator that knows Spanish, Cantonese, and Vietnamese.

The translator also becomes handy in medical emergencies. Tam Dinh says, "Where people are injured, it's always important to get as much information as quickly as possible."

The year 2000 will be the year of e-mail everywhere. No computer will be necessary. These devices from VTech and Cidco plug into any phone line. One button says "get e-mail." Easy. Or you can hook this gizmo from Sharp up to any telephone.

E-books can soon be downloaded into anything: your palmtop or your Rocketbook. Quoting Constance Hale, author of *Sin and Syntax,* "If e-books take off and as a result people read more, great. Because the only thing that's going to make us better writers is to read more and to write more."

The Internet of the future will be less about us talking to each other and more about our machines talking to each other. The refrigerator reads the bar codes on the milk carton, determines when it's time to reorder, and adds it to the Internet grocery list to automatically replenish. Or it might decide to wake you early for work.

The Future of Communications

From a news story by CNN San Francisco reporter Greg Lefevre
January 1, 2000

www.cnn.com

Answers to Exercises: Chapter 1

Exercise 1.1a
Books
Enemies
Thieves
Days
Dishes
Children
Cousins
Wives
Loaves
Cooks
Women
Groceries
Shoes
Friends
Shops
Man
Fishes
Feet

Exercise 1.1b
a. The lady's bag
b. The man's car
c. The ladies' room
d. The men's washroom
e. Cows' milk

Exercise 1.1c
a. Susan-	Proper noun
b. Fish-	Collective noun
c. Students-	Common noun
d. Poverty-	Abstract noun
e. China-	Proper noun
f. Food-	Material noun
g. Group of lions-	Collective noun
h. Family-	Collective noun

i. People-   Collective noun
j. Soil-   Material noun
k. New York-   Proper noun

Exercise 1.2a
a. and nor
b. but
c. or
d. and
e. or
f. and
g. but
h. or
i. or
j. and

Exercise 1.2b
Mary likes coffee but she does not like milk.
Neither Cindy nor Jane is going to the party.
Mary likes clothes and shoes.
You can either watch cable TV or read a book.
Kate likes swimming but she does not like music.

Exercise 1.3a
a. an
b. The
c. an
d. An
e. The
f. An
g. A
h. A
i. The
j. An

Exercise 1.3b
The keys are on the table.
The car is clean.
I need an umbrella.
The computers are on.

Exercise 1.4a
a. goes
b. have
c. is
d. like
e. Studies
f. go
g. arc
h. are
i. have
j. has

Exercise 1.4b
a. went
b. had
c. liked
d. was
e. did
f. went
g. was
h. had
i. liked
j. did

Exercise 1.5a
a. am going
b. is talking
c. are standing
d. is sitting
e. are waiting
f. is combing
g. is cleaning
h. is watching
i. is driving
j. are eating

Exercise 1.5b
a. was sleeping
b. was talking
c. was going

d. were walking
e. was driving
f. were doing
g. were looking
h. was cooking
i. was studying
j. was waiting

Exercise 1.5c
a. went
b. went, liked
c. did
d. had
e. had
f. were
g. saw
h. was
i. did
j. saw

Exercise 1.6a
a. forgot
b. began
c. heard
d. drove
e. felt
f. ate
g. sold
h. saw
i. bought
j. wrote

Exercise 1.6b
a. am sleeping
b. are buying
c. is writing
d. are selling
e. is speaking
f. is choosing
g. is running

i. is eating
j. are driving

Exercise 1.6c
a. was speaking
b. was eating
c. was sitting
d. were beginning
e. were reading
f. was buying
g. was going
h. was sitting
i. was driving
j. was teaching

Adding -*ing* to the verbs

going, sleeping, beginning, running, enjoying, frying, stopping, hiding

drying, sitting, leaving, coming, dying, eating, selling, writing

Adding -*ed*

dried, hoped, bored, died, tried, snowed, cried, needed, believed, called

fried, visited, danced, helped, stayed, planned, rested, wanted, counted, shouted.

Exercise 1.7c.
took
drove
stopped
ate
rested
returned

Exercise 1.7d
1. heard, was sleeping, woke

2. visited, was reading, stopped, spoke

3. cooked, were eating, arrived, brought

4. had, was driving, ran, skidded

5. was walking, started, took

6. went, saw, are, stayed

7. was dressing, rang, answered

8. studied, starting, was working, was

9. did, was doing, came

10. danced, was, arrived

Exercise 1.8a

a. Wine is made by the factory in Germany.

b. They are bored by the history class.

c. He is tired from the gym classes.

d. The garden is being cleaned by him.

e. The plants are being trimmed by him.

Exercise 1.8b

a. They were tired by the walk to the village.

b. They were refreshed by the morning air.

c. She was irritated by the man's singing.

d. The traffic was angering the woman.

e. They were amused by the show.

Exercise 1.9a
a. No, I did not.
b. No, I am not.
c. No, I have not seen Anna.
d. No, I have not finished.
e. No, I didn't.
f. No, I don't.
g. No, I didn't.
h. No, I am not.
i. No, I wasn't.
j. No, it isn't.

Exercise 1.9b
a. did not like, were not
b. did not go
c. did not wash
d. did not enjoy
e. was not happy
f. did not cook
g. did not walk
h. did not pass
i. did not spend
j. did not shop

Exercise 1.10a
a. sleeps
b. sells
c. have
d. have
e. buy
f. buys
g. are
h. is
i. eats
j. eat

Exercise1.10b
a. had lived
b. visited
c. had

d. had
e. sold
f. sold
g. bought
h. bought
i. had
j. liked

Exercise 1.10c

a. is, are
b. is, are
c. is, are
d. is
e. is
f. is
g. is
h. is
i. is
j. are

Exercise 1.10d

a. was
b. was
c. was
d. was
e. were
f. were
g. was
h. were
i. was
j. was

Exercise 1.11a

a. How are you?
b. Where are you going?
c. What are you doing?
d. Whose pen is it?
e. Where do you live?
f. Why are you studying English?
g. How old are you?

h. Where are you going?
i. What time are you coming home?
j. What are you studying?

Exercise 1.11b
a. Where did you go?
b. What did you do on Sunday?
c. Whose book was it?
d. Where did they live?
e. Whom was she speaking to?
f. Who was she?
g. How old was he?
h. Whose house was it?
i. When was the exam?
j. Why were you sad?

1.15 Dialogue. Dealing with a situation.

Complete the dialogue for the following situations. Then practice the dialogue with a friend.

a. Eloisa meets her English-speaking friends at the disco. She wants to introduce her friend Antonio to them. What does she say?

"Hi, Eloisa, how are you?"

"I am fine. I would like you to meet Antonio."

"Wonderful to meet you, Antonio"

b. Your friend from Ireland is visiting you. Introduce her to your parents. Find out where she wants to go and what she wants to do. How long is she staying?

"I would like to introduce my friend. She is from Ireland."

"Nice to meet you. How are you?"

"I am fine, thank you."

"What do you want to do? How long are you staying?"

c. You are at the office. The phone rings. Answer it and find out what the person wants.

"Hello. Good morning. Can I help you?"

"Yes, I would like to speak with the manager, please."

"One moment, please,"

d. You are in an English-speaking country. You need a taxi. Greet a stranger and ask for help.

"Excuse me. Can you help me? I need a taxi. Where can I get one?"

"Yes, you can get a taxi at the taxi stand across the road."

e. Make a simple arrangement by phone to meet your friend for lunch.

"Hello. Can we meet for lunch?"

"Where can we meet? What time?"

"At ten o'clock on Cassanova Avenue."

f. You are at a restaurant, and you don't understand the menu. Ask for help.

"Excuse me, I don't understand the menu. Can you help me?"

"Yes, of course."

g. Call a friend and ask him/her to meet you at the disco.

"Hi, Carlos, can we meet at the disco?"

"Yes, what time?"

"At ten."

h. You are supposed to meet some people at ten o'clock. Call and say you can't make it.

"Hi. I am sorry, but I can't make it."

"Okay, that's fine."

i. The immigration officer at the airport asks you for your address and nationality. Tell him.

"What is your address and nationality?"

"I am Venezuelan. I live at Av. Paseo in Caracas."

Exercise 1.17a
a. at
b. on
c. in
d. on
e. at
f. on
g. in
h. at
i. on
j. in

Exercise1.17b
a. in, in
b. on, at
c. in, in, on, at
d. on, in, on
e. on
f. at
g. at, at, in
h. in, in
i. on, in, in
j. on

1.20. Answers to the Listening Comprehension
a. Sir Isaac Newton was English.

b. He was born on January fourth 1643.

c. His father died three months before he was born.

d. He became a professor at the age of twenty-four.

e. He died on the 31st March 1727.

f. He died in London, England.

1.21 Answers to the Reading Comprehension.
Save the Gorillas

1. The gorillas are threatened by Ebola disease, habitat loss and by poaching.

2. The population of the mountain gorillas is approximately 700.

3. The western lowland gorillas are threatened by Ebola disease.

4. They are increasing due to the dedicated efforts of the WWF.

1.23. Review Exercises
A
1. are
2. is
3. are
4. is
5. has
6. has
7. is
8. is
9. has
10. is
11. are
12. is
13. are
14. are
15 is
16. is
17. is

18. is
19. like
20. is
21. is
22. is
23. is
24. is
25. are
26. are
27. is
28. likes

B
1. knows, is
2. falls, get
3. speak, speak
4. falls, bores
5. needs, is
6. travel, arrive
7. loves, take
8. comes, comes
9. visits
10. feels

C
1. A lot of us are going to the show.
2. Everyone in my class is studying English.
3. The Spanish language is difficult.
4. Spanish people like to dance.
5. Much of the news contains violence.
6. A lot of information is on the Internet.
7. The number of people in the world is increasing.
8. The group of scientists travels everywhere.
9. A large number of people are looking at the game.
10. Many of them watch sports.

D
1. were not, arrived at
2. Isn't, on
3. Aren't, on

4. On, did not go, stayed
5. did not have, got, in
6. do not have, at
7. decided, were not going, remained, in, at
8. was, on, of, in
9. do not have, in, on, at
10. were not, wanted
11. attended, from, to
12. live, in, At, at
13. In, came, on
14. did not like, in
15. at

E
1. T-shirts are being worn by people all over the world.
2. Sodas are being drunk by many children.
3. Wine is being made by many factories in France.
4. The children were being amused by the clown.
5. They were being tired by the lecture.
6. Houses are being bought by many people.
7. The museum is being visited by many people.
8. The game is being watched by everyone.
9. The holiday is being enjoyed by everyone.
10. The trees are being wetted by the falling rain.

Answers to exercises: Chapter 2.

Exercise 2.2a
a. She
b. He
c. It
d. It
e. her
f. them
g. It is mine.
h. It is not yours.
i. It is ours.
j. It belongs to them. It is theirs.

Exercise 2.2b
a. It
b. It
c. They
d. They
e. They
f. They
g. They
h. They
i. It
j. They

Exercise 2.2c
a. has
b. is
c. has
d. has
e. is
f. is going
g. has
h. is
i. are leaving
j. are coming

Exercise 2.2d
a. his
b. his
c. his
d. their
e. their
f. his
g. their
h. their
i. their
j. their

Exercise 2.4a
a. myself
b. myself
c. himself
d. themselves
e. herself
f. yourself
g. ourselves
h. herself
i. ourselves
j. herself

Exercise 2.5a
a. her
b. me
c. her
d. him
e. us
f. her
g. it
h. him
i. him
j. her

Exercise 2.8a
1. whom, who, which
2. whose, which

Exercise 2.8b

a. The lady whose car I borrowed is having lunch.
b. I saw the boy who won the race.
c. I have an aunt whose son is a wealthy businessman.
d. I have a brother who lives in the United States.
e. The book that I read was good.
f. The man whom I met at a party is very rich.
g. He is the man who helped me with my car.
h. This is the computer that crashes all the time.
i. She is the lady whom I met on Sunday.
j. The sound which we heard was strange.

Exercise 2.8c

1.
My father, who spends long hours at the office, is an accountant.
My father is an accountant who spends long hours at the office.

2.
My sister, who is caring and helpful, is a nurse.
My sister, who is a nurse, is caring and helpful.

3.
My brother, who is a politician, is very ambitious.
My brother, who is very ambitious, is a politician.

a. little—adjective of quantity

b. red, yellow—adjectives of description

c. any—adjective of quantity

d. french—adjective of description

e. French—proper adjective

f. This—adjective of demonstration. Our—possessive adjective

g. These, those—adjectives of demonstration

h. much—adjective of quantity

i. Young—adjective of description

j. my—possessive adjective.

a. that

b. these, those

c. these, those

d. this

e. that, this

f. these

g. this

h. that

i. this

j. that

Exercise 2.12a
He is getting older.
He is getting big.
She is getting taller.
He is getting hungry.
They are getting thirsty.
He is getting angry.

Exercise 2.12b
a. better
b. younger
c. tallest
d. best
e. least
f. more
g. richest

h. brightest
i. more
j. fastest

Exercise 2.12c
a. him
b. her
c. yours
d. I
e. I
f. theirs
g. ours
h. hers
i. mine
j. mine

Exercise 2.12d
Big, is, an, she, who, and, can, but, at, to, there, have

Exercise 2.18a
a. next to
b. with
c. to
d. for
e. near
f. by
g. along
h. between
i. among
j. next to

Exercise 2.18b
a. from
b. to
c. for
d. by
e. for
f. to
g. of
h. from, to

i. from
j. by

Exercise 2.18c
a. among
b. me
c. her
d. with
e. for
f. it
g. him
h. him
i. about
j. her

Exercise 2.18d
In, on, her, with, to, him, each other, at, on, at, next to it, on, at

Exercise 2.20b
a. bigger
b. cleaner
c. larger
d. newer
e. more expensive
f. more comfortable
g. smaller
h. bigger
i. more expensive
j.newer

2.22. Dialogue: Dealing with the Situation
a. You are having a birthday party. Call your friend and invite him/her.

"Hello. I am having a party. Would you like to come?"

"Yes, of course. What day and what time?"

"On Sunday at six."

"We will be there."

b. Find out what your friend needs for the party.

"Hi. I am coming to the party. What should I bring?"

"Oh! Anything would be fine."

c. You are at a restaurant with your family. Someone wants a bowl of soup. Ask for it.

"Excuse me, please. Can I get a bowl of soup?"

"Yes, of course."

d. Ask your friend about her/his favorite TV program.

"What's your favorite show?"

"I like sitcoms."

e. Do you have a family pet?

"Yes, I have a cat. Her name is Pepper."

f. You are looking for a house to buy. You meet someone with a house for sale. Introduce yourself and find out about the house. Ask about size, color, how many rooms, and where the house is situated.

"Hello, my name is Tony Simon. Do you have a house for sale?"

"Yes, I do."

"Can you tell me about it? How big is it?"

"It is a blue house with three bedrooms, a living room, a kitchen, and a garden."

"Where is it?"

"In the city. In Sabana Grande."

g. You just bought a new home. What are the things you are going to buy? Tell a friend.

"Well, I am going to buy_____."

h. You are looking for an apartment to rent. Someone has an apartment to rent. Call and ask about it.

"Good morning. Do you have an apartment for rent?"

"Yes, I do."

"Can you tell me about it?"

"It's a two-bedroom apartment that's furnished."

"What is the cost?"

"One thousand dollars a month."

2.23. Answers to the Reading Comprehension
Work Begins at Home
1. A

2. C

3. D

3. B

The Boy from Bogota
a. Marcelo Pino is a young man who is sixteen years old and who is very handsome.

b. He lives in a house that is simple and that has two rooms.

c. One day he was walking home, and he met a lady who was old and poor.

d. He won the lotto.

e. He felt joyful.

f. He ran into the street to look for the poor old lady.

g. He looks for her because he wants to help her.

There Is a Mouse in My House
a. She was very proud of her house.

b. It was always neat and tidy.

c. One day she saw a mouse in her house.

d. She was cleaning the carpet.

e. She told people that mice are never found in her house.

f. She was upset and ashamed.

g. She called the pest company.

h. She asked the man to not tell anybody.

2.25. Answers to the Listening Comprehension
A—reception area

B—director's office

C—secretary's office

D& E—men and women's toilets

F—kitchen

G—accountant's office

H—storeroom

first floor:
laundry area

kitchen
living room
dining room
study area
powder room

Second floor:
master bedroom and private bath
two bedrooms with private baths

2.26. Review Exercises
A
1. himself, who

2. myself, who or that, himself

3. that, which

4. that, yourself, whose

5. who, each other, that, which

6. that, it, our, yours

7. it, her, we

8. ours, hers

9. theirs

10 mine

B

1. I like the car that is very expensive.

2. The man who came to see me is the new English professor.

3. The man whose house I bought is living in England.

4. The blouse which I bought yesterday is too big.

5. The lady whom I spoke to is the new decorator.

6. The teacher who teaches math is very popular with the students.

7. The students who were selected for the trip are leaving on Sunday.

8. The big sofa that I like is very comfortable.

9. I met the man who is the director of the new company.

10. The exam that I passed was easy.

C

1. younger than he
   older than I

2. most

3. more

4. most beautiful

5. taller than I
   shorter than he

6. best dressed

7. happiest

8. driest

9. least

10. less

11. more expensive

12. louder

13. best

14. more

15. better

D

1. for
2. from
3. for
4. to
5. about
6. along
7. near
8. for
9. by
10. at

Answers to exercises: Chapter 3

Exercise 3.2a
a. shining, sunny, sun
b. rainy, rain
c. blowing, windy, wind
d. foggy, fog
e. stormy
f. hot
g. cold
h. falling
i. pouring
j. rainy

Exercise 3.2b
a. hottest
b. higher
c. coldest
d. cooler
e. cooler
f. hotter or warmer
g. hot
h. driest
i. cold
j. coldest

Exercise 3.2c
a. light
b. dark
c. on time
d. late
e. early
f. sunny
g. clear
h. early
i. late

Exercise 3.3a
a. little
b. many
c. very
d. few
e. many
f. little
g. much
h. few
i. much
j. many

Exercise 3.5a
a. can't
b. can't
c. unable
d. able
e. can't
f. can
g. can
h. can
i. can't
j. would

Exercise 3.5b
1. c
2. a
3. b
4. e
5. d
6. f

Exercise 3.5c
Winter, in, their, hot, to, at, sunny, cooler, showers

3.9 Answers to the Reading Comprehension
The Geography of Peru

1. The winter months are June to September.

2. The rainiest months are from December to April.

3. Lima is the capital city of Peru.

4. Cusco was once the capital of the Inca Empire.

Is the Earth Getting Hotter?

1. The golden toad of Costa Rica has disappeared from the forests. Many scientists believe that the toad has been killed off by warmer temperatures.

2. Corals are losing their color and turning white as sea temperatures rise.

Exercise 3.12a
a. since
b. after
c. after
d. because
e. since
f. while
g. after
h. while
i. before or after
j. before

Exercise 3.12b
a. She went to bed because she was tired.
b. The storm started while he was waiting to go home.
c. We can go to lunch after we finish the report.
d. Whenever it is hot, I turn the air-conditioning on.
e. She went to Paris after she finished university.
f. When I was in New York, I saw the plays.
g. Before she goes away, she is going to sell her house.
h. Whenever I travel to England, I take my raincoat.
i. I will travel as soon as I get my passport.
j. We can leave when he comes back.

Exercise 3.12c
1. a
2. b

3. d
4. c
5. e
6. f

Exercise 3.12d
1. b
2. a
3. d
4. c
5. f
6. e

Exercise 3.12e
1. as soon as
2. now that
3. until
4. while
5. as long as
6. until
7. until
8. as soon as
9. while
10. as soon as

Exercise 3.12f
When, while, as soon as, since, whenever, because

Exercise 3.12g
After, before, now that, whenever, because, as long as

Exercise 3.12h
a. as long as
b. as soon as
c. while
d. when
e. whenever
f. since
g. after
h. because

i. before
j. until

Exercise 3.13b
a. Tomorrow I will bake a pie.
b. I will take a vacation next summer.
c. I will go to the shops tomorrow.
d. They will buy a new house.
e. I will sit my exam next week.
f. I will look at television later.
g. I will send an e-mail to my friend.
h. I will go to school tomorrow.
i. He will travel to New York next month.
j. She will cook dinner tomorrow night.

Exercise 3.13d
I will speak to her.
He will buy her a present.
They will send him an e-mail.
She will see him tomorrow.
I will take a message for her.
I will write it tomorrow.
They will see it tomorrow.
She will take him to the zoo.

Exercise 3.13e
a. when
b. when
c. while
d. as soon as
e. before
f. as soon as
g. when
h. after
i. when
j. as soon as

Exercise 3.13f
a. because
b. now that

c. since
d. as long as
e. since
f. because
g. now that
h. now that
i. because

3.15. Dialogue: Dealing with the Situation
a. A major client is coming in from New York. He asks about the weather. Tell him/her.

"It is hot. Very hot. Make sure you wear light clothes."

b. There is a hurricane outside and you cannot get to work. Call and explain.

"Hi. Is this the manager?"

"Yes. What's the matter?"

"The weather is bad. I cannot get to work. It is flooded and the roads are blocked."

c. Invite your friend for coffee.

"Hello. Listen, would you like to go for coffee?"

d. Your friend invites you to lunch but you are unable to go. What do you say?

"No. I am sorry I can't. I have a meeting."

e. You are in a hurry and you need to know the time. Ask someone.

"Excuse me. Can you tell me the time, please?"

f. You need to get some information on courses at the university. Call and find out.

"Good morning. Can I get some information on your courses?"

g. You are at the gas station and you have a flat tire. Ask for help.

"Excuse me. My tire is flat. Can you help me?"

h. You wish to leave work early. Ask your boss for permission.

"Excuse me, Mr. Ross, but can I leave early today?"

i. Your friend is visiting your home. Be polite.

"Please sit down. Would you like something to drink?"

3.16. Answers to the Listening Comprehension
Sun Safety Tips
1. Skin cancer is the most common form of cancer.

2. UV radiation is the most common factor.

3. You should wear a wide-brimmed hat, and you should use sunscreen lotion.

4. The sun affects all ages and all skin types.

Colds and Flu
1. Colds are common in the fall and winter seasons.

2. Colds are most common among children.

3. Hand washing is one of the simplest ways of preventing the common cold. Also, you can avoid contact with people.

3.17 Review Exercises
A
1. can't
2. can't
3. can
4. can't
5. couldn't
6. could
7. can
8. can

9. can't
10. can

B
1. Would you like to sit?
2. Would you care for some coffee?
3. Would it be possible to see him now?
4. Would you like a magazine?

C
1. cooler
2. hotter
3. cooler
4. sunnier
5. warmer
6. drier
7. lower
8. more
9. most

D
1. After I waited a long time at the station, I finally got a train to London.

2. Before I went to Panama, I took a course in Spanish.

3. When I arrived in Lima, it was freezing.

4. I met a wonderful person while I was sitting at the bar.

5. We stood under the bridge until the rain stopped.

6. When I was in Paris, I saw the museums.

7. When I arrived at the office, he was already waiting.

8. Before we went to dinner, we closed the deal.

9. She studies late at nights, after everyone has gone to bed.

10. I waited at the hospital until I was sure everything was fine.

E

1. We can't go to the beach because the roads are blocked.

2. We can't go to the park since it is raining.

3. Now that the roads are cleared, he can leave on time.

4. Since his cat died last Friday, he hasn't eaten dinner.

5. Now that we have money, we can rent a car.

6. Because I am fit, I can run a mile.

7. We can fix the house as long as we have the money.

8. Since he was not feeling well, he stayed in bed.

9. Because he twisted his ankle, he can't walk.

10. We can't go to the meeting because there is a storm out there.

F

1. many
2. much
3. very
4. very
5. a lot
6. little
7. few
8. very
9. few
10. few

Answers to exercises: Chapter 4

Exercise 4.5b
at the side of, next to, on foot, near to, with, at, in front of, cross in front of

Exercise 4.7a
a. The new pharmacy is where she buys her medicine.

b. The old shoe shop is where she buys her sneakers.

c. The blue house on the hill is where he lives.

d. This is the great country from where they came.

e. The new building is where he works.

f. The big bank is where he has an account.

g. The bright city of Las Vegas is where they live.

h. The village market is where she buys her vegetables.

i. The expensive clothes shops at the mall are where she shops.

Exercise 4.8a
a. Christmas is the time of year when we buy gifts for our loved ones.

b. Monday the fifth is when we have our final exam.

c. Sunday is the day when I go to church.

d. I will never forget the day when we got married.

e. Two thousand and one was the year when we celebrated our second anniversary.

f. One in the afternoon is the time when they will arrive from Boston.

g. August is the month when the weather is usually the hottest.

h. Ninteen ninety six was the year when I began university.

i. Tuesday is the day when we have gym classes.

4.11. Dialogue: Dealing with the Situation
a. Your friend wishes to go to the nearest cafe for coffee. Tell her where to go.

"Hi. How can I get to the nearest cafe?"

"_____"

b. A tourist wishes to change money. What do you tell him/her?

"Can you tell me where I can exchange money?"

"Yes. You can change money at the bank"

c. You get a call from your friend who is at the airport. Tell him/her how to get to your home.

"Hi. I am at the airport. How can I get to your place?"

"_____"

d. You lose your bank card and credit card. What do you do?

"I have lost my bank cards and credit cards. What can I do?"

"You should go to the bank immediately and let them know."

e. You need information about a money transfer. Ask the bank clerk to help you.

"Good morning. Can you help me check my money transfer?"

f. You are in a foreign country, and you don't know the bank hours. Ask someone.

"Excuse me. Can you tell me the bank hours here?"

g. You are a salesperson in a store. Greet the customer and find out what he wants.

"Good morning. How may I help you?"

h. Your friend wants to buy a child's dress. Tell her what to do.

"You should go to the City Mall."

i. You buy a pair of shoes, but they do not fit well. Take them back and ask the salesperson for a new one.

"Excuse me. I need to exchange these shoes. They do not fit me well."

j. You need to get apples and grapes at the fruit mart. Ask for the items and find out how much each item costs.

"Good morning. I need some fruits: apples and grapes. Can you tell me the cost?"

4.12. Answers to the Reading Comprehension
The Internet Reborn
1. More than 600 million people use the Internet worldwide.

2. Twenty-four percent are Brazilians.

3. Seventy-two percent of Americans go online once a month.

4. Scientists are trying to replace the Internet with a new model.

4.14. Answers to the Listening Comprehension
1. Cell phones will be small enough to hide in your pocket.

2. E-books can be downloaded, and people could read more.

3. If you can't speak the language, no problem. Automatic translators are on the way.

4.15 Review Exercises
A.
1. bought

2. paid
3. asked
4. went
5. opened
6. spent
7. shopped
8. fitted
9. changed
10. visited

B
1. was buying
2. was paying
3. was asking
4. were going
5. was opening
6. was trying
7. was waiting
8. was walking
9. was running
10. was exercising

C
1. I thanked the shop attendant who was helpful to me.
2. The jacket which I liked was very expensive.
3. The manager whom I met on Sunday is sitting in the room.
4. Today is the day when they will come.
5. The blue house is where she lives.
6. The car that I saw was not good.
7. What he said was interesting.
8. The man whose house I live in is sitting there.
9. Thursday is the day when I go to the gym.
10. The new office building at the corner is where she works.

D
1. whenever
2. until
3. as
4. when
5. as soon as

6. before
7. after
8. while
9. as soon as
10. whenever

E
1. because
2. as long as
3. since
4. now that
5. because
6. now that
7. as long as
8. since
9. now that

F
1. little
2. few
3. any
4. some
5. any
6. all
7. all
8. all
9. many
10. many, all